EMBRACING THE PORCUPINE

GERMAINE SMITH

THE CENTER FOR HEALING PRESS

© 2024 by Germaine Smith. All rights reserved.
ISBN: 978-0-9960421-7-8 (print).

Library of Congress Control Number: 2024905149

All rights reserved. No portion of this publication may be reproduced or transmitted in any form or by any means, electronic or mechanical, including photocopying, recording, or capturing on any information storage and retrieval system, without permission in writing from the publisher, except by a reviewer who may quote brief passages in a critical article or review to be printed in a magazine or newspaper, or electronically transmitted on radio, television, or the Internet. The Center For Healing Press is the imprint of The Center For Healing, a spirituality center of education and prayer for those seeking wholeness.
For reprint permission: germ@thecenterforhealing.us.
Front Cover picture by Germaine Smith

All rights reserved.

Dedicated with deep gratitude to my spiritual companion
    on the journey:

Paul Deziel.

Thanks for walking with me.

WITH ABOUNDING GRATITUDE:

Connor Blacksher
Mary McPherson

PREFACE

The challenges of every life are not the exterior forces but the internal ones: the demons within. In her book "*Eastern Body, Western Mind*, Anodea Judith expounds on the Hindu chakras, the seven energy systems that govern the body and soul, and identifies a demon for each chakra. These are not demons outside us but our own feelings, attitudes, old tapes that motivate, overwhelm, and paralyze us. This adversary or demon emotion is our most challenging teacher, inviting us to confront ourselves through owning and feeling our own pain and suffering.

I have added an assistant to each adversary named by Judith. Both are instructors: inviting us to confront ourselves through welcoming wariness, appreciation for lessons, and finally, gratitude.

CHAKRA	ADVERSARY[1]	ASSISTANT
1. Grounding	Fear	Courage
2. Creativity	Shame	Honor
3. Power	Guilt	Humility
4. Love	Grief	Gratitude
5. Communication	Lies	Honesty
6. Intuition	Illusion	Wisdom
7. Union	Attachment	Surrender

Anodea Judith, *Eastern Body, Western Mind*, (Berkley, CA: Celestial Arts, 2004). I have reversed the second and third chakra demons.

The style of this book is modeled on the ancient Hindu spiritual classic, The *Baganda Gita*. The *Gita* explores a conversation between Prince Arjuna and Krishna, an incarnation of the god Vishnu. Arjuna is anxious about an upcoming battle in which he will fight against his kinsmen.

Krishna lays out the spiritual and practical reasons why Arjuna should fight by delving into dharna, karma, reincarnation, and the quest for Enlightenment.

Some scholars propose that this conversation is not really between two individuals but the dialog each person must have with him or herself. The "fight" is not outside but inside. It's the battle within. The battle between what one wants and what one needs. The battle between the head and the heart. The battle between the ego and the True Self.

We all face this battle of wrestling with ourselves. The winner determines the direction of our decisions and ultimately, the outcome of this life.

0. THE PATH

I

It's nice to meet you, Sage. I'm not sure if you can help me, but my life is falling apart. I am so lost. I just don't know what to do. Things can't get any worse! I feel as low as I have ever felt. I am truly at the bottom. I know I sound crazy. I have been unhappy before. But not this bad. Not this hopeless.

I had always thought advisors, spiritual guides, therapists were for other people. After all, the miserable shape of the world is evidence that lots of folks need help. Other folks. Lots of other folks. Just not me.

Don't get me wrong; I know I am not perfect. I just never wanted to bare my soul in that way. Don't want to bare my soul in any way. But my life had never been this bad before; I had never felt this barren before. There must be more to life than feeling worn out, desperate, empty, and afraid.

Perhaps you can help me. Rumor has it you help folks figure out their issues and get their lives back on course. Well, my life is so off course, I am ready to try anything.

SAGE

Thus lies a grand and harrowing adventure before you. The journey to healing. All life is the journey to wholeness, one in which there are no shortcuts, no effortless bypasses. It is a path fraught with challenges and confusion. Most folks don't walk this path until they have exhausted all other routes.

The great teacher Buddha used the analogy of swimming to describe this adventure. Expanding his parallel, I believe there are four main stages for each of us to choose from and eventually work through.

Many of us stay inland, totally unaware that that a great body of water even exists. We focus and remain in the material world: making money, having families, staying busy, unaware of the spiritual aspect of all creation. It will take many lifetimes to realize there is a shoreline.

Some of us will realize there is a shoreline but refuse to enter the water. We prefer to play upon the sandy beach. The journey to wholeness begins when we are brave enough to enter the water.

Water has often symbolized our emotional state. Entering the water means we are willing to face all those wounds we have denied. Some of our wounds are decades old; some inflicted just yesterday. Until we are ready to face all our injuries and embrace them, we remain wounded. Healing is the task of every single person on the planet. Because the reality is: we are all wounded.

Entering the waters of emotion to face ourselves, we confront our denial and admit our woundedness. Some of us will only wade in, refusing to go into the murky depths. We admit our pain but go no further. This is a good start but not enough.

Full healing is only possible when we are brave enough to swim beyond the shore. This is terrifying for us: we can't touch bottom and the waves of painful emotions are daunting. We're afraid will be swamped, pulled down until we are sucking silt on the bottom. Yes, there will be times we feel like we are drowning. But we will re-surface if we persevere. We will ride the waves of our emotion until we are one with the water. Then and only then, are we one with ourselves.

It is a hellish journey but one the brave take because on the other side is paradise.

Are you willing to begin the swim to healing?

THE ANALOGIES

I

I know I am complaining and I know it's only been a short time but I don't feel like I am making any progress. I try and try but I keep falling back. I had several great days: my attitude was positive; my mood was lighter. But it didn't last. Maybe I cannot do this. Maybe I am not ready.

SAGE

Only you can decide because only you can walk this path. If you run away today, the path will simply wait for you to return. There is no escape. You can walk away but the lesson remains. Remember, the path of healing is never a straight one. Sometimes, analogies help demonstrate this reality.

For the first analogy, consider the design of a metal spring. It curves forward until it bends and starts to move backward. After reaching the bottom of its descent, it turns and climbs up and out, advancing ever so slightly forward. It reaches the apex again only then to coil back down again. It repeats this pattern over and over again as the spiral lengthens. It is the same with the movement of life.

We have good days when we are climbing high and life is full of promise. The light is bright and the sun illuminates everything. Then things start to fall apart as we start to descend into the abyss and the bottom seems endless. Darkness grows deeper and deeper and there appears no way out.

But then there is. The dawn breaks through and we find hope rekindled. We also discover we are not in the same place as we were before. We have inched forward a bit in strength, confidence, wisdom.

We want to stay on the upswing, with the light brilliantly upon us. But that is not how life unfolds. We will go back to the darkness. Because darkness is the place of growth It is easy to believe the absence of light to be some sort of evil. It is not.

The darkness is a place of germinating who we really are by confronting our demons. Not exterior demons but the ones within our own hearts and minds.[2]

Darkness can be very scary. It is easy to get stuck in the darkness if we let go of hope. Many of us spend our lives stuck because of fear or despair or exhaustion from fighting the darkness. So how do we handle the darkness?

We embrace the darkness by developing curiosity. What does my anger, shame, fear offer me? What can my guilt, ungroundedness, paralysis teach me?

The second analogy is "the house." We all have a karmic house with many rooms, containing all aspects of our life. There are rooms for family life, work life, educational life, etc. There is also a room for our wounded life. This room we have locked away, never to be seen again, all our pain and suffering. Healing demands we must open the door and enter.

Some of us will never open the door, choosing to live in denial and therefore, in pain. Some of us will only clean a small part of the room. We mistakenly believe that vacuuming the carpet but leaving the rest of the room untouched, makes the room clean. Unfortunately, does not.

To heal, we must clean the room completely: move everything down to the studs. That means removing the furniture, tearing down the walls, ripping up the floors. Then we can rebuild: put down new flooring and construct better walls. Decide what furniture we want in

---

[2] Mohandas Gandhi.

this room instead of the unhelpful or damaged furniture someone else has given us.

Another analogy is that of a garden. To make a garden you must first clear the land of all debris. But that is not enough. For plants to grow, you must dig deep into the earth, plucking out the roots of weeds and breaking up rock-hard lumps of dirt. Then your seeds have a tender, tilled bed in which to take root. To heal one must root out all that is harmful, not just cutting it off at the surface.

The final analogy speaks to the healing of a physical injury. An untended cut on your forearm will become infected. Once infected, it doesn't matter how many band aids you apply — the infection takes hold. Even a hundred band-aids cannot heal the wound. The wound must be opened, lanced, drained, and cleaned for recovery to occur. If left to fester, this once small wound may end up killing us.

Our emotional wounds are akin to our physical ones. They need to be opened, lanced, drained, and cleaned for healing to occur.

As you can see, healing is a jagged journey with twists and turns. There will always be an excuse to run away, a compelling rationalization for not doing the hard work of healing. As your teacher and guide, I must own my limitations as a human being. Perhaps there is another path to wholeness. But honestly, I don't have any idea what that might be. This is the only way I have found that healed my wounds: face the demons inside me.

So, what is your decision? Are you ready to begin again? And again? And again? And again?

FEAR & COURAGE

EMBRACING THE PORCUPINE

I

My boss is such a jerk! She wants me to do cafeteria duty! ME!! I am a high school teacher, not a baby sitter for rowdy teenagers having lunch. But what can I do? I have no choice in the matter! This may seem like an inconsequential problem to you but it makes me so hot. It is so unfair!!

SAGE

Life is easy when life is good. The real question is: what do we do when life is difficult? Let me tell you a story from my own experience.

My work schedule at Target starts at 4 AM. One year, some corporate executive decided that to save money, no one could start work before 7 AM. Everyone at my store agreed this was a terrible idea: no way to get our store ready to open if we could not get in early to accomplish this task. I voiced my protest to everyone! But of course, to no avail.

Finally, realizing that bitching about it served no useful purpose, I decided I had to embrace this new schedule. One day, my boss approached me to ask how I was doing. I admitted I was struggling to embrace the new start time. To demonstrate my point, I spread my arms out in an imaginary hug. He asked if it was like trying to hug an elephant. Bluntly I said, "No. It's like trying to hug a porcupine."

Humans like to fight the porcupine. Despite the reality that the quills inflict wounds upon us. Erroneously we believe two things. The first is that by doing battle we will change the porcupine. We do not have the power to change the porcupine. No matter our efforts, the porcupine will remain a porcupine.

Our second erroneous belief is that we are somehow honorable in this fight. This battle does not make us noble. Some battles do. But not this one. It's not noble to continue to fight something you can't change. It is however, a great form of insanity!

This fight will always have one sure outcome. Between the claws, the teeth, and the quills, we will be bloodied and more wounded than when we started.

Embracing the porcupine means you stop trying to change the people you cannot change and start working on changing the person you can change: you. You can change your attitude, your approach. You can do the unthinkable: make friends with the porcupine!

This takes courage because fear is the most powerful motivator. It seizes us, screaming out "Danger! Stop! Go no further! Go back! Don't change!" We give in to the old message, retreat into old habits, stuck in the darkness of fear.

Seeking to avoid any confrontation with fear, we mistakenly believe that we will avoid our pain. Truth is, only through courage do we realize that fear is our greatest teacher. Fear is always inviting us to a direct, face-to-face encounter. An encounter with ourselves.

Embracing the porcupine means doing the opposite of what we have done in the past. It means doing the reverse of what all those voices in our head scream at us. Then despite our shaking and trembling, we embrace the porcupine: admit our fears, then walk toward them. Because embracing the porcupine, my friend, is the key to healing. And healing is the key to enlightenment.

MOUNT EVEREST

I

A friend of mine is stuck on several significant issues right now. When I told her what you have said about facing one's issues, she replied point-blank: "I don't want to feel the pain." Instead, she told me about a new healing technique in which one does not need to go into their pain for it to be released. Perhaps she's on to something. Perhaps there is an easier way to heal than having to face the pain directly.

SAGE

Perhaps. But while your friend's approach may be helpful, it does not address the root cause of most issues. This time I will use the analogy of ascending Mount Everest. Your friend is trying to take a helicopter to the top; I want to climb every inch of the way up. You may wonder: Why choose the harder path?

Indeed, both methods get you to the top. But climbing Everest teaches you something you can never learn in a helicopter. Climbing the mountain teaches you who you are.

If I had not faced my horrific childhood abuse, I would never know my strength, courage, or worth. If I had not recovered from all sorts of addictions, I would not intimately know my defects as well my gifts. Learning who I am is the gift of climbing the mountain.

Yes, the journey of ascending Mount Everest is fraught with peril. But the rewards of facing our fear and ascending to the top are vast. Climbing our mountains introduces us to our essence: our dignity, our integrity, our wholeness. It teaches us who we are at our core. You can't learn that in a helicopter. You can only learn that by climbing up the mountain, one step at a time.

THE DMV

I

This was the worse experience of my life! I think I just need to tell someone the whole sordid tale because I am so distraught. My driver's license was due to expire in June. With all my paperwork in hand to get my enhanced and my doctor-approved restricted license, I headed to the Edina DMV on May 8. As you know, for many years, I have had a restricted license because of my eye diseases.

All went very perfect. The wonderful employee scanned in everything then gave me my temporary license. But by the middle of August, I still had not received my new license. So, I called the DMV: three different phone numbers and three different departments. One hour and fifty-three minutes later, the reason: no record of my doctor's paperwork. I told DMV employee that I had indeed watched the form being scanned when I applied for my license. But she did not believe me.

I get it: she couldn't believe me. She needed the form as proof, not my assurance. But panic started to set in. It made no logical sense, but panic often doesn't.

I told myself to calm down; there was an easy solution for this. Just have my eye doctor fax the form over to the DMV. Problem solved. When I called the office, I was told the fax would happen immediately. Wonderful! Calm restored.

Thirty minutes later, the office manager called me back. No one could find my forms for the DMV. Panic refueled. And it was loud! I was not going to get my forms in on time. My new license would not arrive before my temporary one expired. I would have to drive illegally; I might even get arrested. The worst fear of all was that I would lose my license. Forever!

I knew these thoughts were irrational but couldn't stop them. I had to get this fixed immediately before these dire consequences pounced upon me. The best solution was to drive back to Edina, even though without an appointment, the wait would be long. But I had to hand them my only copy of my form personally. So, at 9:58, I arrived at the DMV and got my number for all the folks without appointments. C 37, by the way. There were fifteen numbers ahead of me. Forty-five minutes later, the countdown was down to three. I felt pretty good. The panic was manageable and I thought within thirty minutes, C 37 would, certainly, be called.

Unfortunately, none of the walk-in numbers were called during the next forty -five minutes. That's when panic won and I unraveled.

At first, I felt anger. After all, I had done nothing wrong. I had brought all my forms in on time. I was a good citizen. But none of that mattered. I was not in control, feeling powerless, helpless, and trapped. So, sitting in my plastic chair at the Edina DMV, I could understand why people get violent. Not wanting to fuel my anger, I decided to let go of my anger. That's when I started to cry. As the tears of hopelessness ran down my face, I did try to conceal them but not to stop them.

Finally, C 37 was called. At 2:02, I walked out of the DMV with the assurance that my license would be sent immediately. After 105 days, I got my license!

SAGE

I'm glad you got your license, but that's not the important part of the story. What was really going on? What is the lesson from the DMV? What made you so panicked? It was the terror of being broken.

Every one of us possesses a state of being in which fear has no power. I call it the core of being. This is where I stand in my true Self, accepting of all I am, loving all I am—unconditionally. Fear, shame, guilt, pain have no power because I am whole. And I know it.

The core of our being is always present but often inaccessible because of our fear and our wounds. We don't believe we are good enough, whole enough. Then we run away. Ultimately, we run away from our true selves.

For a long time, I felt that I was terrified of being me. The fear of what I would find if I looked inside paralyzed me. The longer I remained paralyzed, the more the fear dominated. Then the Universe provided me with an invaluable opportunity to face my primal fear. That is what the DMV is offering you: to learn a foundational lesson from fear.

When I was a child, I was broken many times by my father and mother. Through sexual abuse, rape, threats, beatings, and torture, I knew the process of being broken. It often began with words that tore me down, followed by the actions that bullied, humiliated, violated my body. These actions resulted in the stripping of my self-esteem and self-worth, and culminated when I would beg for them to stop. Begged. Not asked or requested. Begged.

Your process might vary but the results are the same: being left powerless, hopeless. Even worse than that, it left me dead inside. For a long time, I thought they had stolen my soul –I was that empty.

They didn't, of course. But that is the horror of being broken. I believe that this is every single person's greatest fear: that she or he will be broken. Left with nothing. Powerless. Hopeless. Feeling like someone stole the very essence of life. It doesn't matter if one has had a good life this time. Traumas from our past lives cast long shadows.

So, we do everything we can to avoid being broken. We escape through all sorts of addictions to deny the very possibility that we could be broken. We try to control everything and everyone, falsely believing if we break others, then we will not get broken ourselves.

This fear is so primal, so ancient. It is everyone's great fear. And one that must be faced if we wish to heal. Faced and embraced as the part of humanity that we don't want to admit.

At some point, I got tired of fear being the victim. Lots of folks think not being the victim means they must be the perpetrator. Not true. Those are two sides of the same coin. There is another path to take. One where you are not the victim nor the aggressor. This path takes courage but it is the only one that leads out of the cycle of fear and pain.

I decided that finding my core and healing was worth facing all that fear had to offer. Healing meant facing my fears. All of them. Healing meant fear would no longer run my life.

I was hoping to find something worthy of the effort. What I found was a sacred, beautiful Self.

That is what each person will find when she or he courageously searches for the core of being. A sacred, beautiful Self that is inviolate to being broken.

CLAIM TICKET

SAGE

Now is the time to re-claim ourself.
We give ourselves away sometimes rather easily.
Our task as adults is to re-claim ourselves:
    from all the people, groups, and entities
    that we have given ourselves away to.
Then and only then, can we consciously know who we are.
Then and only then, can we stand in our power
    and stand as one with the Power of the Universe.

I got claimed by everyone else.
    My dad wanted my will.
    My mom wanted my conformity.
    The family wanted my silence.
    The church wanted my obedience.

There was no room for me;
No room for me to stretch out; no room to be myself.
That ends today.
I need to break the chains that hold me.
Those chains are not me;
    they just bind me to old patterns and sickness.

So today and every day, I re-claim myself.
I own me. No one else.
I am in charge of my decisions. No one else.
My acceptance of myself is what matters No one else's.
What I think of my efforts is what matters.
    No one else.

I re-claim all of me,
    the gifts as well as the defects I possess.
I'm not perfect and that's more than enough.

FEAR AND ADDICTION

I

What kind of a question is that? "Have I examined my addictive behaviors?" I'm not an addict!

SAGE

The Buddha said that the main addiction of humanity is the addiction to me, myself, and I.[3] We are all addicted to getting what we want. All of us. What we want is to be safe from this great fear of being broken. Our fears stem from a simple construct: we will lose what we have or we will get what we don't want.

Then we choose a particular addiction to escape from that fear. For some, addiction is external: drugs, sex, video games, shopping, gambling, greed, OCD, etc. But there are also internal addictions: controlling others, egotism, perfectionism, rage, greed, abusing others. Mental addictions are just as powerful as physical ones.

Addiction is easy to detect. It is a thought-process or behavior we cannot stop, that numbs us or distracts us, or is unhelpful to our wholeness. I have a huge list of addictions in my life: drugs, alcohol, control, arrogance, self-righteousness, rage caffeine, sugar. I could go on but you get my point.

The pattern is the same. I sense discomfort—something is not going my way. Because I am afraid to admit it or feel it, I run away to avoid the discomfort. Running away is antithesis to healing. I cannot heal if I am running away. So, take the first step: admit which views or actions are unhelpful to you but you cannot stop them. What thoughts or behaviors render you powerless?

---

[3] Pema Chodron, *Don't Bite The Hook*, Shamballa Audio, December 2017, disc 1.

LIVING INSIDE

I

Okay. I have examined my addictions and yes, there are a few thought patterns that are quite unhelpful. But as I was reflecting, I had the most peculiar feeling. I felt like I was living outside my body. I could feel myself outside my physical body; my soul just in front of my chest. Have you ever experienced anything like this?

SAGE

Absolutely. This feeling of not being in one's body is the direct result of our addictions. No matter what the addiction, the outcome is always unconsciousness. Living outside one's body.

Unconsciousness is the reality you are describing. When I am unconscious, I am not "in"; I am "out". When I walked; I felt like my body was always trying to catch up with my soul. When I talked with folks, I was always answering before they even finished speaking. The more I became aware of my additions, the more I could feel this phenomenon.

I was living outside my body because it felt safer. Ultimately however, it was more dangerous. Unconscious decisions are not the wisest because they are often fear based.

Living in one's body means one has integrated body and soul in the heart chakra. We are then connected to both Earth and Divine energies, which of course, is what we humans are. Earth and Divine. We are present, fully alive, whole human beings when we live integrated in the heart. And let's face it, that is very scary sometimes.

In facing my fears, I face myself. As with all things, practice is the key. The easiest way to practice is to simply invite your soul in.

Stop. Settle. Breathe. Invite. Repeat.
Often.

WHERE ARE THE BODIES BURIED?

SAGE

We all have buried parts of ourselves out of fear.
Call them out from the graves of denial and avoidance
       from the graves of powerlessness and victimhood.

I called mine out from the tomb
       where I buried hope and joy and safety
       covered with freshly turned farm dirt.
From the woods
       where I stood with a .22 rifle leveled at my chest
       ready to end all my pain.
From the barn
       exchanging the smell of rape
             for that of straw and cows.
From the freezer
       filled with ice cream and chocolate chip cookies
       that served as my sole comfort
             after being tortured.
From the bottle and bong
       that saved me from killing myself more swiftly.
From the fantasies of heroically saving myself
       out of my hell called childhood.

I call myself home from all the places
       I buried parts of myself.

Come home.
It is safe now and I welcome you back with open arms.
Come home.
I will see you, honor you, love you, protect you.
Come home.
We can be whole again.
We can be one again.
Come home

THE PORCUPINE OF FEAR

I

I have worked with my fear for a while now but it still is quite strong. Sometimes, it is so overpowering that I just give in. There are times when I feel like I am being stalked. Fear creeps around me, waiting and watching. Other times, I feel like I am being actively chased and pursued. Whether my fear is creeping or attacking, it just won't go away!

SAGE

And it never will go away. Not completely. No one can eliminate fear. The point is to face fear. To stand still as it creeps around you; to not run away as it advances full steam toward you.

Thus, with fear all around you, you do the next right thing. Yes, you are still afraid but you move forward anyway. Because you have decided that that there is something more important than fear. Your body. Your mind. Your soul. Your integrity. Your sanity. Your dignity. Your very being. And when you realize you are more important than fear, then you refuse to let fear dictate your decisions.

The bottom line is that we courageously face ourselves despite being afraid. Fear may be present but it is no longer in control.

SHAME & HONOR

THE BIRTH OF SHAME

I

I don't know the answer to your question. I'm ...I'm... I'm...I'm...I'm... I am struggling right now. I don't know what to say or what to do. It feels like I can't find any ground. I feel like I am spinning and I can't stop it. I've tried and tried and tried to do the right thing in life. But I just feel like a failure. I can't explain this! Feel so stupid! So embarrassed!

SAGE

That is the voice of shame. Shame tells us we are so horrible, so undeserving. That we must remain silent lest all the world realizes exactly how pitiful and disgusting we are.

Of course, shame is a lie but it has been repeated and reenforced in so many ways throughout our lives that we have swallowed all its falsehoods.

I was ashamed of my childhood and the horrific abuse that was my daily diet. As a child, I was taught I was to blame for all the beatings and rapes and neglect and unlove. I believed that I was the bad person in my family.

I was ashamed every time I was broken. Ashamed that I had lost my identity and knew I would lose it again. That made me feel so weak and powerless. I was ashamed that I had lost hope again. Lost my strength and confidence again. Every time I was broken, I was nothing. Again.

Shame is thrust upon us by another person. Then we carry the burden ourselves. Shame's voice is another person's voice that we internalize as our own.

A lot of our shame comes from parents who were unable to fill our self-esteem bucket. But it can come from anyone. A coach, a teacher, family member, neighbor, clergy, a friend. Anyone who tells you are not good enough, not worthy enough, not sacred, not important.

I

If shame is from an earlier time in my life, why is it so strong now? After all, I am an adult. I successfully teach a classroom of teenagers every day. But your question just rattled me so much. Right now, I feel like I have a sign on my back that screams: LOSER.

SAGE

Because shame is internalized, we carry it with us. You just got triggered by my question. Truth is, the cause of shame is not the same as the triggers of shame. Shame develops when someone believes we have disgraced them; then they tell us or shows us that we are unworthy, undeservingly, insignificant, useless, unlovable. Their words or actions demonstrate that they are embarrassed by our very existence. The reality is that the embarrassment and shame is theirs. But they can't admit it. So, they throw it at someone else. At us.

A trigger is when someone says something that may be totally unrelated but exposes our shame. My question had nothing to do with shame. But it tore off the band-aids you had covering it. You got triggered. You felt ungrounded and confused because part of you traveled back to the event of your shame. Every time we get triggered, we lose our bearings.

Then you did a very wise thing: you admitted you were triggered. You didn't use that word but you expressed the feelings. Most folks pretend nothing happened. Which of course, doesn't help or heal anything!

My shame started at a very young age. As I got older, shame remained as my constant companion. As you know, my childhood was treacherous. I was raped and beaten repeatedly by my father. I desperately wanted by mother to protect me but all she did was try to pacify my father. Usually by focusing his anger and attention on me!

I felt so worthless and unloved that for most of my life. I just wanted to die. Despair, desolation, hopelessness, isolation are the expressions of shame.

I

But I wasn't raped or beaten. I don't think I was even abused. And yet, I sure feel the words you are describing. They reside deep within me.

SAGE

One does not have to have been raped to feel shame. I was ashamed of being an addict because I thought it confirmed my weaknesses. Ashamed of my employment at Target because I believed I was too good for the job. Ashamed of not fitting in, not having many friends. All my shame verified my unworthiness. The truth was I was ashamed of me.

I felt so inept. So indecisive. So pathetic. Shame keeps us from living our own lives. I have a friend who admitted a powerful truth about himself when he said, "I was living my wife's life." Because of our shame and our fear of that shame, we live someone else's life. Which means we aren't living at all!

We exist in the exterior of our being rather than living inside. Our shame keeps us from realizing that living on the inside is the only place we will find peace.

Now that we have defined shame a bit, let me ask you my question again. Perhaps this time it will be easier to answer. How did you celebrate your birthday?

I

Yes, I think I can. The answer is I don't really celebrate my birthday. Haven't in decades. I view it as just another day. No big deal. No celebrations. No focus on me.

Emotions are so weird, aren't they? You are right: your question had nothing to do with shame and yet, everything to do with shame. It triggered me back to when I was seven. Isn't that nuts? I haven't thought about this incident since it happened. Yet you ask an innocent question and bam! Suddenly, I am seven years old. Standing in front of my birthday cake. Tears streaming down my face. With my mom screaming at me!

My parents had just had another gigantic fight about me. They got divorced when I was two and since then, spent most of their time arguing about my custody: who got me, when, where, and for how long. Each of them at various times plowed right over the court issued custody schedule.

On my seventh birthday, this particular argument was because my mom got offered this big promotion at work. Problem was she would have to move to Chicago. She wanted me to live with my dad for the school year and she'd take me for the summers. A proposal he adamantly refused.

Then I spilled punch all over the floor. I thought she'd hit me; she was so mad. She ordered me to sit at the table and as she was cleaning the floor, she started shrieking, "Why did I even have kids? You've been nothing but trouble since the day you were born. I wish I never had you. I wish you hadn't been born." That's when I started to cry.

Later, she apologized and told me she didn't mean it and repeated how sorry she was. We made up and life went on. But I could never allow myself to celebrate my birthday after that. It was easier to pretend it was just another day.

SAGE

I am so sorry that happened to you. I'm sorry she took out her frustrations on you. You did not deserve that. I'm sorry she blamed you for her life's challenges. And I am sorry that you internalized her messages.

You are not responsible for her job. Or for her decisions or disappointments. Or for your parents' custody issues. You are not responsible that she is a parent! You are the result of her decision. Not the cause of them.

That is the essence of shame. Someone throws messages at us that are not ours. We take in those messages. Winterize them. Own them as if they were ours. But they are not. They are someone else's messages of frustration. Of pain. Of woundedness.

SHAME LIES

SAGE

We are all wounded by shame. Wounded by hurtful words, painful actions, or empty silences that shred our confidence, stole our hope, stripped our honor, and dismembered our wholeness. Here is the first lie of shame.

Because of our painful wounding, we run away. Run away and try to believe the seductive and false promise that denial of our shame will make all our problems magically go away and life will be happily ever after. This is a gigantic lie!

Lie number two. We believe the shame. On some level, you believed you were to blame for you parents' problems. You were too much work for them, too much trouble for them. Then any normal mistake you do, like spilling the punch, gets magnified. So now, you are not only the useless and unwanted kid but you are the horrendous screw-up who can't do anything right.

Lie number three. We try to control the fall-out of our shame. I bet that you have spent a good deal of your life trying to be perfect so that you could keep the shame in check. If you can do everything perfect, perhaps the voices of shame that tell you that you are unworthy and unlovable will be quieter. This doesn't work. You are a human being and therefore by definition not perfect! Trying to be perfect only adds more pain.

Lie number four. This one is another form of control but I think it deserves its own category. We change our lives in order to minimize the pain shame causes us. You stopped celebrating birthdays. Perhaps to punish yourself. Perhaps to avoid re-living the memory of your mom's condemnation. Perhaps hoping to avoid future shameful event. Perhaps all the above.

If we don't know how to heal the shame, we try to change everything else. In your case, you stopped recognizing your birthday. But by eliminating a joyful celebration, you did not heal your shame. You just reduced your enjoyment of life.

Lie number five. You said your mom apologized. That's good. We all lash out and say hurtful things when we are hurt ourselves. Then we do need to apologize and seek forgiveness. That is our opportunity to re-built the relationship.

The lie is when we believe that the apology will always erase the shame inflicted. Sometimes it does. Sometimes it doesn't. For whatever reason, shame has penetrated to a very deep level and an apology is not enough. This is not the other person's responsibility if his or her apology was sincere. We are responsible to dig down to find the roots of our shame in order to heal it.

Lie number six. We believe we can move forward, carrying all our shame with us, unhealed, without any ill effects. Can't happen. Won't happen. Doesn't happen. Shame keeps us stuck. Stuck in despair. Stuck in self-hatred. Stuck in emptiness. tuck in hopelessness. Stuck.

CREATING HOPE

SAGE

"It's not the past that broke you, it was the empty future." I don't know who said that but it is powerfully true. We got broken: sustained an emotional injury that steals hope and confidence Some wounds are like hair-line fractures. They are painful but with patience and gentleness, we heal ourselves.

Some wounds are compound fracture with both bone and spirit shattered. We are devastated, lost. This is terrifying because not only is there no hope in that present moment, we feel no hope for the future.

Hope is essential for life. "Hope is oxygen for the soul."[4] A necessity. At the end of virtually every therapy session, I would ask some version of the same question: "Is this pain going to end?" In the midst of my emptiness, I was searching for hope. And the answer, patiently given, each time was: "YES!"

When you are unable to offer hope to yourself, find another to help you. This doesn't mean they do your work for you. It means they hold the light of hope when you are lost in the night. And all they need to say when you ask the question, "Will this get better?" is "Yes."

Hope is oxygen for the soul because hope allows us to believe, to know that each of these statements are truth. We can heal. Our pain can end. We have worth. We are important. Life can be fulfilling. We can know joy.

---

https://others.org.au/news/2021/07/19/hope-is-like-oxygen-for-the-soul/ (accessed December 20, 2022.).

HONOR

SAGE
Repeat these often. Even if you don't believe them!

I have honor and dignity
    no matter what I have done
    no matter what others have said.

I am loveable.
    Always and forever.

I am worthy of good things in life.
    I am worthy of happiness.
    I am worthy of love.
    I am worthy of having people in my life
        who treat me with respect.

I am whole
    even if I don't feel whole.

I deserve to be here.

I am responsible for me.
    I am NOT responsible for my parents.
        Or any other adult.

I am important.
    I am important to me.

GUILT T & HUMILITY

GUILT THE NOUN

I

I just read a historical account of a young woman arrested for heresy during the Inquisition. It was terrible! She was hounded and questioned repeatedly. Then was beaten because she would not confess. Can you believe it? These so-called leaders of Christianity were nothing but thugs. Finally, she was executed—burned at the stake! For a crime she did not even commit! So utterly ungodly and inhumane. What a betrayal!

SAGE

Yes. Human history is filled with the effects of our guilt. We all make mistakes and hurt others and ultimately hurt ourselves. This is reality. The real tragedy is when we do not learn from our past. When we do not admit our errors. Most of us drape ourselves in denial, cover our misdeeds anyway we can. Then we pretend we are in the moral right. But I am sure you didn't come here today to talk about issues that happened centuries ago.

I

Well...this chapter of history really bothers me. It is so senseless. The church officials were supposed to service justice, not thwart it. They were so evil in their disloyalty!!

SAGE

Yes. But the more interesting question is why, this historic episode that happened centuries before you were born is bothering you so much? Often, we get triggered by events that have no obvious connection to our own lives and we react with great emotion. Something happens that opens an old wound that we thought we had completely buried. Your emotional reaction is a great clue that you are triggered. So, what has this story from the past uncovered for you? What is it bringing to the surface?

I

I guess it's because my best friend is having an affair and got caught. She and her husband have been together for years but he is an abusive man who treats her horribly. Even so, I am so angry with her for blowing up her life this way. She betrayed her vows. She should have left him. Not cheated on him.

SAGE

Both your stories are about betrayal. Why are you so judgmental? Sounds like you have your own wounds regarding betrayal. What happened?

I

Well.... Yes, I guess I do. But I really don't want to talk about it. Bringing it up and reliving it won't help anyway. No one can change the past. I have never told anyone because it's too terrible. You see, no one betrayed me. It was I. I was the traitor.

SAGE

No matter how many deeply we bury it, to avoid facing it, guilt doesn't go away. It remains a wound, alive under all the hand aids we have used to cover it. It remains, waiting to be healed. Because all our guilty wounds are alive, they fester and infect the rest of our being. Some of those wounds are inflicted by others;

some of them inflicted out ourselves. Truth is, all wounds need to be healed regardless of who inflicted them.

"Self-care is how you take your power back"[5]. When we deny and bury guilt, it confiscates so much more than we realize: our self-respect, self-worth, integrity, peace of mind. Self-care demands we face our guilt so that it no longer holds our power.

You started today by being angry at others' who betrayed their standards. That is projection: you don't want to deal with your emotions so you thrust them onto someone else. The person you are furious with is yourself. Begin the healing now. Tell me what you did.

I

I just can't. It's too hard. If I tell you, you'll know what a horrible person I am. What a hypocrite I am. That I really am a LOSER.

SAGE

Let me tell you a little about guilt. Guilt is the belief one has committed a wrong Synonyms include: indiscretion, culpability, sin, fault, failing, mistake, error, transgression, misconduct, maleficence. One may feel: remorse, regret, self-condemnation, loathing. One may pretend to feel nothing but the emotions of guilt remain.

Under normal circumstances, guilt is the natural occurrence when I cause physical, emotional, mental,, or spiritual harm to myself or another. Put another way: guilt results when I have an attitude or commit an action that violates my true Self.

Another way to look at guilt is through the lens of karma. "Guilt has very long-reaching tentacles. Disturbing the life of another will disturb your life;

---

[5] Judith, *Eastern Body, Western Mind*, 143.

destroying the life of another will destroy your life."[6] Thus, guilt must be dealt with honestly and completely, or it destroys you.

Unlike shame, guilt is ours. Because we are responsible for causing harm; we must take responsibility for the wounds we have inflicted.

Now let me address this feeling of yours that yours is the worst wickedness. Believe me, everyone thinks their most horrible actions are worse than anyone else's. They aren't. We are all the same: we all screw up. In incredibly destructive ways. Most frequently, we seriously hurt those we love the most.

We all do the same things. We lie, cheat, steal, betray, rip others apart. In the words of Kahlil Gibran: "If we sat in a circle and confessed our sins, we'd all laugh at each other for our lack of originality." In the end, there is one grave and vital reason for us to tell the whole truth about our transgressions. Until we do, we carry the heavy burden of guilt around with us and that will inevitably lead to loss of self-respect and ultimately end with self-hatred.

The choice is yours: self-hatred or truth?

I

This is so difficult for me to tell. I feel so guilty. But you are right: I hate the way I feel. So maybe telling you will help.

About ten years ago, when I was teaching at another school, I began stealing. Little things at first. Office supplies, books, food from the cafeteria. Stuff like that. I was really struggling to make ends meet at the time and I knew the school would not miss the few things I was taking. At the time, I felt like I deserved to help myself to a few vital essentials. After all,

---

[6] *The Dhammapada*, edited by Kenneth Easwaran, chapter 10.

Catholic schools don't pay much. So, I was just making up for my inadequate salary.

Then I stole some computer equipment. I didn't think anyone would notice a couple of missing iPads but the tech team did. The school investigated and accused a math teacher. They told him if he made restitution, they would only put a letter of reprimand in his file but not fire him. So, he paid for the I-Pads and I thought the issue was history. I was so relieved because I knew I would get fired if anyone found out it was me.

SAGE

Thank you for trusting me. It is always an honor to listen as someone shares their story. Admitting what we did wrong is the first step. But admitting is not enough. We need to repair the damage we caused. We need to make amends. Without fixing it, the guilt remains. And that means the self-hatred remains.

Let me repeat: confession is not enough. You must make amends. That means fixing, in some appropriate manner, what you broke. I used to steal a lot when I was using drugs. When I became sober, I sent money to everyone I could remember that I stole from. Sometimes, anonymously. Sometimes, I signed my name. But I repaid it all back with interest.

In fixing things, we can be very creative because there are countless options. Sometimes, we need to confess to the person directly. Sometimes, in order to protect another person, we must act indirectly. Let your conscience be your guide. Your Greater Self will tell you which path to take. That is the only way to deal with guilt. So, how can you fix this?

I

That will definitely take a lot of creativity because the math teacher died in a car accident a couple of years ago. But his family requested donations be made to his favorite charity; I can give money to that.

SAGE

Great idea. Do that and then see if your conscience is calm. You will know if you need to revisit this. Just remember: if it is not settled, it will tug at you until you fix it. Burying it will only prolong the misery of guilt. And believe me, guilt is a misery! The good news is we don't have to carry it around with us any longer than we want to. When we are ready, we can let it go.

The flip side of guilt is humility. Humility is the art of embracing our humanity: our assets as well as our defects. We all screw up. We all hurt others and ourselves. Humility teaches us that when we accept ourselves fully, no matter what injuries we caused, we are redeemable.

GUILT SIDE EFFECTS

SAGE
You seem distant today. What's troubling you?

I
Nothing. I just have a lot of on my mind. Work is very taxing right now; it's a very busy time for my students. I probably should have skipped this time with you. I don't really have much to say.

SAGE
That sounds like denial. Well, since you don't have much to say, let me talk for a bit. Last time we talked about guilt, I did not tell you about all the side effects of guilt. Let me elaborate on all the ways guilt can affect us when we bury it.

Guilt is a burden that reaches out from the grave to destroy us. Much as we try to deeply bury it in some unmarked region, guilt refuses to stay hidden, refuses to stay silent in its persistence to be embraced and owned.

I know "embraced" is a strange word for dealing with guilt. But that is exactly what we must do to avoid the plethora of side effects that guilt brings.

The first side effect of guilt is that it restricts the free flow of movement by eliminating joy[7] Thus, it is not possible for us to be happy and be guilty at the same time. That fact alone should propel us to face our misdeeds! When we cannot experience joy, there is a void within us. We feel restless, empty, desolate, unfulfilled without joy. To make things worse, we try to fill this void with all sorts of other stuff that will never satisfy or fill us.

---

[7] Judith, Eastern Body, *Western Mind,* 119.

Compulsive behaviors develop from this "hunger" we cannot fill. We eat, drink, smoke, shop, zone out too much to compensate. Want to know the insane part? We keep repeating the unfulfilling pattern even though we are left so unsatisfied.

The second effect of guilt "is that it is "the prison that keeps the shadow caged"[8]. Our job as adults is to integrate the many personality parts into our "indivisible whole." To be integrated, one must face all the aspects of one's self.

We all have a "shadow" side. Our shadow is all our repressed, unconscious energies. This includes all energies we believe are "bad." Like anger, sexuality, shame, being lazy, being too loud, being too quiet, pain, grief, power, pride, etc. Anything we think or have been taught is "wrong" lives on in our shadow.

Denial keeps the shadow in the prison of guilt and "robs the whole of grace and power"[9] And believe me, the shadow will not remain silent. It will come out in all sorts of unhealthy ways.

The reality of energy is: what is put our attention on, grows. The more I bury my guilt, the more I will draw it back to myself. A great example is when you reacted to the story about the church's betrayal. Your guilt came back to you via another story about guilt.

The law of energy is: what we focus on, increases. Then we make a logical mistake. We think if we do NOT focus on something, it will go away. I erroneously believe if I deny my shadow side, if I deny my guilt and pain, it will stay buried, away from exposure. But that is not the way energy works. Denying, burying, minimizing, running away are all futile efforts. The energy remains. But not dormant.

---

[8] Judith, *Eastern Body, Western Mind*, 119.
[9] Judith, *Eastern Body, Western Mind*, 119.

We are on this planet to learn and our shadow side is our teacher. Remember, whatever we try to avoid will find a way to reach us. You focused on the Church's shadow in order to avoid your own. So, you get mad at the Church for its betrayal and the lesson is to realize that you are angry at yourself.

A third effect of guilt is closely related: self-righteousness. We are often very critical and judgmental toward our shadows. After all, our shadows are the parts of ourselves, we don't like. But because we cannot admit our shadows, we project them onto others. That judgement is our clue of the rejected self. Whenever we focus our righteous indignation at someone else, we are avoiding our own fear and guilt.

This is a very common pitfall: we condemn someone else so we don't have to confront our own shadows. I have been guilty of this more times than I can count. Do you know why I am so vehement about condemning another shadow? Because another's shadow and mine are the same! Your antipathy of the Church's butyral is really your antipathy of your own betrayal. The lesson is: anytime I am self-righteous, I need to look honestly and conscientiously at my own history.

One of the most challenging and harmful side effects of guilt is that it polarizes the personality. It is the source of dualism where we believe there are only two options: good vs. bad, right vs. wrong; reward vs. punishment.

Dualism presented itself many times in your situation. From the very beginning when you were deciding to steal, you thought there were only two options: deprive yourself or steal. Then again when the tech team started investigating, your two options: remain silent or confess. And then again at the end, appear innocent or get fired. Guilt reduces matters to black and white. In reality, most issues are gray.

Guilt's side effects, like ripples in a pond, carry us further and further away from our True Selves. Despite the fear and embarrassment of our guilt, owning our actions is exactly what we must do if we wish to transform guilt into joy. There is no way around guilt. The only way is through.

All parts of the personality need to evolve and that happens through expression of all aspects of ourselves. You have spent years pretending this event didn't happen. When that didn't work, you projected it on to the Church, still denying your shadow. In the end, you compartmentalized yourself. But that is not healthy. Healthy is integration.

Facing the shadow is facing all our hidden needs and wants in order to channel them appropriately. Facing our shadow allows guilt to be seen and evaluated so that all parts of our being are reconciled with each other. Then we are whole. Again.

THE PORCUPINE OF GUILT

I

Just like you said, I was hoping it would go away. It's so bad I couldn't face it. And my conscience has been tugging at me. I can't sleep. I can't eat. I am riddled with guilt! I need to tell you the whole story.

Obviously, you remember when I told you about my stealing and the math teacher who was accused of my theft? The truth is, I planted evidence so he would get blamed. I got so afraid the school would suspect me, I left all sorts of clues to point, not only to someone else, but specifically to this math guy.

I am so sorry! I feel so terrible! At the time, I didn't think the school would fire him because he was so popular and beloved by the administration. That's why I chose him to take the blame. He was always such a suck-up, always doing everything right. But if I got caught, I knew they would fire me.

But now, I feel so horrible. I am so sorry! It was a rotten thing to do. And now, there no way to fix it. Donating money didn't help much and he's dead. So, I'm left with all this guilt and no way to fix anything.

SAGE

This is an important lesson for you. Remember everything is about learning. Not right or wrong. And guilt can always be dealt with; guilt can always be healed.

Let me summarize. When we cause pain to ourselves or another, we can choose to stay stuck in denial, rationalize our behavior, and play the victim by blaming someone else for our mistakes. This choice is common to all humans. We choose denial so we don't have to feel our guilt. We rationalize in hopes that we can minimize what we did. We blame to avoid responsibility. These attitudes spin us into self-pity. That's where you are now: feeling unforgiveable and hopeless. But these are all futile efforts that ultimately lead to despair. Because if the guilt is ours, it is not going anywhere.

Facing guilt is never easy. But facing it is an absolute necessity. "Unresolved guilt is the autoimmune disease of the soul because it literally rejects our own worthiness as human beings."[10] And none of us need an autoimmune disease!

These steps bear repeating.
1. Accept that the event happened. Take responsibility for it.

2. Analyze the motive. Why did you do it? Dig deep to understand your actions lest you will repeat them. Remember the context of the situation. What I did when I was thirteen needs to be viewed differently than what I did at thirty. This is not a "get out of jail" free card but an acknowledgement that the severity and depth of guilt changes depending on maturity, authority, age, responsibility, motive, etc.

3. Apologize. We must admit our guilt out loud to another. That's the only way our guilt gets relieved.

4. Make appropriate amends. This means we fix what we broke. When appropriate, we make amends to the party we offended. When that is not possible, we get to be creative. The only exemption is if our amends would cause greater harm.

You only dealt with part of your guilt and part of your amends. Admitting half our guilt still leaves half. Now you need to finish.

---

[10] Joan Borsenko

I

But I don't know how to finish. Yes, I already feel so much better by telling you the whole story. But how can I fix his reputation? And how can I make amends to a dead man?

SAGE

I had to make amends to my boss and did not want to do it. So, I tried to side-step direct amends in all sorts of ways. I offered prayers for her. I gave money in her name. I confessed to another person. I promised myself it would never happen again. But none of that was not enough. I kept feeling my guilt. Finally, I picked up the phone and apologized to her directly.

Perhaps you cannot restore the math teacher's reputation directly but you could tell his family how valued he was and how dishonest you were. You could tell your story to others as an example of confession and humility. Truth is, there are a great many avenues open to you. When we listen, we know what needs to be done. Right now, you know what you need to do; you don't need me to tell you. Listen to yourself and find your courage. Then do it.

We always know when our guilt is healed —we stop feeling guilty! And there is no better feeling than having the weight of guilt removed from us and replaced with the joy of embracing both our shadow and our light. That is the joy of being humble!

GUILT GIFTS

SAGE

We do not think of guilt as having gifts but it does. Guilt shows us where our boundaries are and where boundaries are absent. When you placed the blame on the math teacher, the gaps in your honesty and ethics were exposed. Reflecting on your gaps gives insight into your own wounding and awareness of what you need to work on next.

Our guilt shows us who we really are. When you project the image of an honest person but then steal, your guilt displays your hypocrisy. Then guilt allows you to reflect on that behavior to determine who you really want to be: the honest person or the thief.

Dealing with our guilt builds our self-respect back from the ashes of self-hate. Apologizing and making amends demonstrates maturity and integrity. These actions announce our growth, healing, and wholeness.

Facing our guilt provides the opportunity for us to re-learn how to get our needs met. If we don't want to repeat our unethical behavior, we must learn a different way. You can learn to get what you need without resorting to unscrupulous or wounding behavior, like stealing, lying, and betrayal.

When guilt is buried and denied, it is a relentless demon who steals our hope for self-worth and joy of life. When guilt is faced and owned, we humbly embrace who we truly are: humans with talents and limitations, persons with light and shadow. "Then guilt is not a demon but a gift."[11]

---

[11] Judith, *Eastern Body, Western Mind,* 121.

GRIEF & GRATITUDE

WHAT'S LOVE GOT TO DO WITH IT?

I

I have a question that sounds so easy to answer but it is not. At various times in my life, I knew the answer but now —frankly, I just don't understand. So, I'd like to hear your opinion. What is love?

SAGE

What a grand question! I appreciate your preface to the question. At times, we all feel like we know everything about love; other times, love is a complete mystery.

Love is so much more than an emotion. Love is a commitment. A way of life. A human necessity. A spiritual goal. Let me paraphrase one definition from Paul of Tarsus. Love is patient, love is kind. It does not dominate or bully; it fosters and encourages. Love does not envy, it does not boost, is not rude, nor self-seeking. In fact, egotism, is the antithesis of love. Love keeps no record of wrongs. It is not judgmental but tolerant with good boundaries. Love does not delight in evil but rejoices with the truth. It always protects, always trusts, always hopes, always perseveres. Love never fails.[12]

I

Sounds nice but a bit remote. How do you define love?

---

[12] First Corinthians 13:4-12.

SAGE

To me, love is cultivating and nurturing my own growth or cultivating and nurturing another's growth. Hatred is anything that interferes with my growth or another's.

I

Hatred? Really?

SAGE

Yes. I know hate a strong word. But one either loves or hates. You see, hate is the absence of love Hate is when love is shut out, closed off. Most often, we refuse to love because we have been hurt. Our pain hurts so much, we consciously or unconsciously withhold our love. In order to protect ourselves from future pain, we limit love from others and limit love to others. This deep sorrow from loss is grief. And we cannot talk of love without talking about grief. Because to love means we will experience grief. To have our hearts be open to love means we will get hurt.

Grief is deep pain caused by loss. Someone's death is an obvious example but loss has many expressions: loss of safety, relationships, illness, desire, career, security, stability, hope, childhood, physical mobility, innocence, sharpness of mind —to name a few losses humans experience.

Grief numbs us to emotion and aliveness. Let me give you an example. The first time I fell in love I was twenty-six. When the relationship did not work out, I was devastated. Devastated because I had opened my heart so fully and then felt so rejected. I no longer felt safe being authentic.[13] So I shut down. Closed my

---

[13] Judith, *Eastern Body, Western Mind*, 272.

heart so I wouldn't get hurt in the future. I didn't want to feel that kind of pain again.

But closed isn't healthy. Closed isn't living. Being numb to love also shut out other emotions. So, I wasn't alive. Wasn't vibrant. Because I wasn't feeling. You see, the primary reason to have a human body is to experience emotions. So, when I closed my heart, I wasn't truly living. I was just a shell.

In my twenties and even my thirties, I still had a huge amount of unresolved grief from my childhood. Growing up, I thought love was striving every minute to earn my parents' affection. It was doing everything "right" so that they would value me Mostly, I believed love was not getting raped or beaten.

I think this happens to most of us: we don't deal with childhood loss, unaware of the grief and sorrow within. And the next loss we experience, feels even bigger. And it is because our grief is multiplying.

So, at twenty-six, when my first love didn't work out, I was just crushed. All the pain from the break-up piled on top of all the sorrow of my childhood. It hurt so much, I never wanted to love again.

I

Did you fall in love again?? How did you open your heart?

SAGE

Yes, I did. By embracing the porcupine of grief.

GRIEF RUN AMOK

SAGE

Before I elaborate, let me tell you a little more about the effects of grief. We all experience loss: someone we love gets cancer; we didn't get the promotion we wanted; the love of our life breaks up with us. The lesson is to deal with it the same way we deal with fear and shame and guilt. Feel it. Own it. Embrace it. Then heal it.

But sometimes, when confronted with loss, we refuse to admit it. This happens a lot in relationships. The energy, the love is gone. But we cling to the other person, wanting love to return. Hence, we stay with someone much longer than is healthy. Doing this produces three results. One, denial just increases our grief because the longer we hold onto something that is gone, the greater the grief. Second, often our clinging just results in resentments on both sides. Third, and most importantly, our denial closes our hearts and emotionally shuts us down.

It's hard to let go because it means facing our loss and our grief. An episode on a television series summed it up very well. Rusty, the teenager who had been abandoned by his alcoholic mother, said, "I thought she loved me. And letting go of that is what is so hard." To which his guardian responded, "But holding on to someone who is already gone is even harder."[14]

When we refuse to deal with our grief, all sorts of things run amok. Obviously, our denial hurts our own well-being. But it ripples from us to infect the world because buried grief often leads to hatred and hatred often leads to evil. Hatred is the absence of love and

---

[14] *Major Crimes* Television series, "Medical Causes", TNT, 2012.

evil is the intentional act of harming another or yourself. And we do it all the time. All of us.

Unresolved grief, like shame and guilt, demands to be owned and will escape from the bunker where we have tried to contain and bury it. It will take one of two avenues of expression: self-hatred or as hatred toward everybody else.

Self-hatred shows up as depression, self-loathing, being critical of every action we perform, perfectionism, refusing to accept compliments, seeing only our character defects, condemning ourselves. Self-hatred is a no-win, bottom of hell place that needs to be escaped from the second you realize you are there!

Hating the world is the other common detour from dealing with our grief. Sometimes at the object of our love but more often, we rage at everyone and everything around us. We think that our fury will fix our grief; mistakenly believe that being rageful will stop the pain. Notice I used "fury" and rageful." It's okay to be angry at loss. But when we get stuck in anger or it turns to rage, we become hateful and evil actions usually follow.

Almost every evil action we experience in our world can be traced to unhealed grief. School shooting, domestic murders, bombings, greed, ethnic cleansing, war. "One who thinks that by causing pain to others, he will have any pleasure is tangled in the bonds of hatred."[15] Refusing to admit loss, denying grief all too often leads to blame, rage, and violence. Then, no longer the victim, we have become the perpetrators. For thousands of years, we have known the truth but been unable to stop our patterns of human cruelty. That truth is very simple. Admitting the loss, dealing with the grief is the path to

---

[15]. *The Dhammapada*, edited by Kenneth Easwar, 21.

healing and the path back to love. Then we heal ourselves and thus, heal the world.

I

I can't imagine healing the world right now. I don't feel like I can heal myself. I asked you the question about love because my partner and I split up a few months ago. For a while, we fought all the time. Then we didn't fight at all. Didn't even speak to each other. We both knew it was over and the split was amicable. But I didn't realize how much it still hurts. I don't really want the relationship back but I am really grieving the loss of hope that it would work out and I'd be happy.

THE PROCUPINE OF GRIEF

SAGE

Even amicable losses are still losses. And all losses produce grief. There are many great books written on dealing with loss that may help you navigate these waters. For today, let me give you the highlights of healing grief using your relationship as an example.

Admit the loss. And there will be many, great and small. Going to the movies alone, the empty place at holidays, the way your partner smelled after a shower, making love the first time, making love the last time. And yes, the loss of hope is a great loss. Let yourself feel the weight of all those losses. But don't let that weight keep you at the bottom.

Embrace the pain, feel it, then let it go. There are unlimited ways of releasing losses from our grasp. Discharge them unto Mother Earth. Write out the losses and burn them in the Fires of Change. Pour them to the Rivers of God. Print them out on toilet paper and flush them down the commode. Know that everything, everything, has a beginning, a middle, and yes, an end. When that end comes, release the grief, holding onto cherished memories.

Remember the lessons learned and the joy celebrated. Your partner taught you how to laugh, how to cry, how to love. Glean all the lessons learned from your relationship. Death cannot take away the experiences you shared if you face your grief.

Feel the grief and then, let go of the person or situation with compassion. No matter how much pain you feel, no matter the level of your resentment at the break-up, offer blessings and good will to your partner. Know she or he is on another part of their journey. A journey that does not include you. Let your mantra be: "I wish you great happiness."

Grief has its own timeline. So, be gentle. It will not be gone quickly. Grief will present itself at the most inopportune times, in the most unlikely places. Years from now, a question on *Jeopardy* will bring you back to that bar in London where you and your partner celebrated your birthday. And even though years have passed, this random question on television will still produce a stab of grief. Though it lessens in intensity, grief lasts a lifetime.

Know with certainty that grief will ease if you face it. It will not consume you. Know with certainty, the pain will lessen. It will not take giant steps but rest assured, there will be movement forward. Life will resume; you will find a new normal. Know with certainty, that life is unfolding as it should. Each person has a path to walk that we may not understand and definitely don't control. And know with absolute certainty that the pain will transform to gratitude. It will take time but at some point, if you face your grief, you will laugh again. You will find joy again. You will love again.

So now, let me answer your question of how I opened my heart again. The short answer is — I had an affair. With myself!!

HAVE AN AFFAIR
[WITH YOURSELF]

SAGE
I sought many things from the outside to fill me:
      food, drugs, alcohol, people, job, approval,
      position, popularity, applause.
This unproductive, barren, futile effort always
    always
      led to a magnum amount of grief.
Because nothing from the outside of me can fill me.

Healing the grief of my little kids and my adult means
    I learn to fill myself from the inside.

I am likeable. I am immensely liked by me.
I am loveable. I am totally loved by me.

I have value. I have priceless value to myself.
I deserve respect. I have eternal respect for myself.

I am worthy. I have infinite worth for myself.
I am important. I am vitally important to me.

I acknowledge and release
    all the pain and grief I have acquired.

Today, I take responsibly for filling myself.
No one else can do this for me.

Today, I fill myself with me.
And I am enough.

LOVE GRANTED

I
So, if I own my grief and love myself, I can heal from loss. Is that your point? And then what??

SAGE
Yes, that is my point. Because you can only love another to the degree you love yourself. If you love yourself a little, you can only love another a bit. And the reverse is true also. If you only love others a bit, you are only loving yourself a bit.

If you deeply care for yourself, you then can deeply care for another. And then, you can love better. And when you love better, you live better.

I
So, I am back to: what is love?

SAGE
Love is the intimate act of sharing who you are. That is why loving yourself is so important. You must know who you are and accept yourself as you are: gifts, defects, assets, and short-comings. Filled with self-acceptance means filled with self-love. Only then can you genuinely share yourself with another and appreciate when another shares who she or he is with you.

Intimacy is bringing forth the deep, vulnerable, sacred, interior aspects of one's self. My friend said it best when we met for lunch last month. I asked him a very personal question to which he responded, "I will answer you because I want you on the inside of my life."[16]

---

[16] Christopher Ranweiler, conversation with author, November 22, 2022.

Simply brilliant!! So, love is inviting others into the inside of your life. And love is when others invite you into theirs.

Problem is, intimacy often terrifies us. Reacting, we refuse to let people in but pretend we are. Fear wins and we shut the door to vulnerability. Usually because we are afraid of being hurt again.

Other times, we hang on to the relationship far too long and then waste precious energy. The other person denies us intimacy but we refuse to admit it. They have closed the door to closeness but we keep banging and banging on it, pleading that they re-open the door. But no amount of pounding will work because we cannot change another.

My responsibility is to speak and listen, honestly and authentically, in all my relationships. Analyze and then clearly state what I want and need. Then I need to listen, not just to the words but the actions of the other person. If we both can get our needs met, wonderful. If we need to part because we cannot meet each other's needs, so be it. We separate as gracefully and honorably as we can. Then we deal with our grief.

I

And how do I do that? I'll just get hurt again! My partner used to harp constantly that I didn't l listen. Wasn't paying attention. I felt so worn down by the time we ended, I was so glad to be out of the war zone.

SAGE

Love always means pain and hurt are a possibility. But the alternative is closing your heart. And that absolutely means you will be a shell. Not alive. Opening your heart does <u>not</u> mean you are a doormat for your partner. It does <u>not</u> mean you are a bully either. Opening your heart means you love with good boundaries.

SPACE: THE FINAL FRONTIER

SAGE

Feeling rejected by my family, I discussed it with my therapist. She said, "You want to be part of their world. But they are not making any space for you in it."

Love means making space for others in your life and being offered space in theirs. Making space means you invite people into your heart. You are willing to be exposed and vulnerable. And the other person is willing to do that also. Making space means you accept the whole person — not just the parts that you like or make you feel good or get you want you want.

Making space happens to different degrees depending on the relationship. But whether a casual friend or close confidant, the process is the same. We make space for others. If they interfere with our growth, we assess. Violations certainly include physical harm but more often it is the emotional or spiritual harm where we need good barriers.

The goal: to be respected, honored, listened to, wanted, appreciated, valued, accepted. These are the essentials of a healthy relationship. Now let's be honest, healthy relationships take work, effort, conversation, and negotiation. We seek to make it work for both parties. But if someone refuses to make space for you, it's time to build boundaries and re-evaluate.

Notice "space" can be helpful in two ways. One, another wants us to be part of their life and they make space for us in it. Two, someone interferes with our well-being and won't make space for us in their world, then we set boundaries that give us space <u>from</u> them. Setting boundaries is not a mean or cruel action. It is a mature response to a harmful or toxic attitude or behavior. Our health and well-being demand it!

HEALING THE HEART

I

I tried to love my partner. But I hated getting picked apart day after day. I don't know if I was ever invited into her world. I ended up bitter. And very resentful. So, I want my boundaries to be very strong so I don't repeat this pattern again. That's healthy, right?

SAGE

As we all know, relationships don't always last. At least not the way we want. It is so painful when there is no space for us. We feel rejected, unworthy. Often, we don't respond by setting boundaries; we react by erecting up walls that would rival any medieval castle!

Massive walls do keep others out but they also keep me barricaded inside. It is very hard to have compassion or empathy for others when I am insolated by walls. Walled off and walled in. Perhaps there are one or two folks who are so toxic that we need massive walls to guarantee our protection. But that is the exception, not the rule. The majority of our boundaries needs to be more useful and balanced.

I use the image of boundaries between my property and neighbors. Depending on the boundary needed, options range from a row of hostas to a short hedge to a picket fence to a chain-link fence. This gives me great flexibility in adjusting the barrier as the relationship dictates. If we reconcile, I can open the fencing up. If we continue to hurt each other, I can make it stronger.

Play with boundaries. Practice setting, holding, and re-adjusting them. As you do that, you demonstrate to your heart that you can and will protect yourself. And knowing that, you can then heal.

HEALING THE WORLD

SAGE
Ready for the hard part?

I
No, not really. But tell me anyway.

SAGE
Our challenge is to love ourselves and fill ourselves from within. Hold good boundaries to demonstrate that self-love. Then we make space for everyone. Yes, we make space for all those we like. But we also make space for all those we do not like and those who don't like us. That's the beauty of good boundaries. I can still wish someone I don't like great happiness. I just do it from a distance.

I
You want the truth? All this talk about love has brought up so much pain. I don't even want to make space for those I like. Certainly not for those I don't like. And to hell with those who don't like me!!

SAGE
That's because you are in pain right now. But you are not going to stay in pain. You don't want to live in pain any longer than absolutely necessary. You want to heal your pain so you can feel again. Remember that is the primary reason for being human: to feel! We all need to keep that goal in mind so we don't get stuck in the muck of grief and despair.

I
Well, I don't think I want to love even from a distance. Even that feels too risky. But I do agree with you. My massive walls do keep others out but they keep me locked inside. I just don't know if I want to take them down. Yet.

SAGE
There is one emotion that counters all our resistance. Gratitude. I was taught that gratitude is the most healing emotion.[17] That's because, "gratitude is not only the greatest of virtues, but the parent of all the others."[18] This is important. Because the answer to grief is gratitude.

I
I don't feel grateful. It feels so empty being alone. I am so lost and completely out of hope.

SAGE
Feel all those emotions. Admit them. Own them. But don't wallow in them; don't get swamped by them. One way off the bottom is to remember the gifts your partnership brought you. Or another option is to consider what opportunities that ending this relationship might bring. Know that is not an unloving action. It is simply the acknowledgement that everything has a beginning, a middle, and an end. And following every end, is another beginning.

---

[17] Mary Bergeson.
[18] Marcus Tullius Cicero, https://www.goodreads.com/quotes/72368-gratitude-is-not-only-the-greatest-of-virtues-but-the#:~:text=%28
(assessed February 3, 2023)

                I
    Still, I don't feel grateful. I don't think my
relationship brought me any gifts. And I'm not sure I
even want another beginning. My life sucks. Everything
is so hard and bleak. I have no gratitude for loneliness!

               SAGE
    But there is gratitude for loneliness. You just
need to find it. Remember this is a learning planet.
Everything has a lesson. You see, learning is the key.
And learning to be grateful is the greatest key.

FOR ALL THINGS

SAGE
In all things, are teachings and learnings. Especially the difficult challenges of life. And if we are reflective, we will find both the lessons and the gifts nestled in our hardships.

I am not grateful for being raped
        but for the strength to not only endure it
              but recover from it.

I am not grateful for being broken over and over again
        but for the resilient spirit
            that the breaking honed.

I am not grateful for a childhood spent in fear
        but for the self-reliance my childhood demanded.

I am not grateful for my loss of innocence
        but grateful for the maturity and depth
            needed to endure.

I am grateful for all the lessons taught by my abusers.
They showed me through violence
        the path I did not want to travel.

Despite the memories that scar my body, mind, and heart
        I am grateful for my childhood.

I am not grateful for the disease that took my sister
        but for the gift of family that she brought me.

I am not grateful for two eye diseases and loss of sight
        but for the ability to adapt and trust.

I am not grateful that my chosen career path has stalled
        but for the opportunities to let go of control.

I am grateful for all pain and despair
        that taught me empathy and compassion
        for the entire world.

I am grateful all the things I planned
        never materialized;
        those losses encouraged me to let go.

I am grateful for an adulthood spent searching for God;
        I learned surrender and submission.

I breathe in gratitude for a life of struggle and strife
        and yet —
        the holy wonders of dawn
        and sacred birth of personhood
        and the absolute beauty of being.

I am who I am because of all my experiences.
And for that, I am very grateful.

UNKNOWN GRATITUDES

I
I'm sorry but I still feel like I have nothing to be grateful for. I can't see anything good: only loss and disappointment and pain and emptiness.

SAGE
You're right. Sometimes, life is so difficult it's hard to find anything to be thankful for. That's when I try to remember this: "If you can't be grateful for what you've received be grateful for what you've escaped."[19] Because, no matter what the circumstances, my life could be worse. Much worse.

This lifetime, I am grateful, I escaped homelessness,
    of living in shopping carts and cardboard boxes.

This lifetime, I am grateful I escaped a life
    of being uneducated and illiterate.

In this lifetime, I am grateful I escaped a life of hunger
    dumpster diving for other people's garbage.

This lifetime, I am grateful I escaped unheated housing,
    outdoor plumbing, toxic drinking water.

This lifetime, I am grateful I escaped unemployment or
    physically challenging and mind-numbing jobs.

This lifetime, I have escaped major physical disability
    confined to wheelchairs or other machinery.

---

[19] Unknown.

This lifetime, I have escaped serious mental illness
    that often further separates human beings.

This lifetime, I escaped the path of utter loneliness
    where no one shows up to help.

This lifetime, I have escaped the ravages of war
    and all the destruction that follows battle.

This lifetime, I have escaped imprisonment
    for crimes committed.
This lifetime, I have escaped unjust imprisonment
    for crimes not committed.

This lifetime, I have escaped government oppression,
    labor camps, military coups, and overthrows.

This lifetime, I have escaped inhumane employment in
    sweatshops, prostitution rings, and forced labor.

This lifetime, I am grateful I escaped repeating
    the ideology of violence.

This lifetime, when I cannot be grateful
    for what I've received
    I am grateful for all I have escaped.

LIES & HONESTY

THE FIRST WHY:
THE IMPORTANCE OF TRUTH

I
I'm fine. Not much going on in my life. I have been very busy lately: school, painting my living room. I even bought some new bookshelves that I must put together. That'll be fun! So, life is good. I'm doing fine.

SAGE
You don't look fine. Neither your face nor energy match your words. And I get it. Often when folks ask how we are doing, they are just being polite. But the truth is important. It's vital that we don't lie to others and imperative that we don't lie to ourselves. Because lies have far-reaching consequences.

I
I wasn't' really lying to you. It's just easier to tell people what they want to hear.

SAGE
Lying often appears easier than telling the truth. But that's just denial. In my experience, lying is not only harder but incredibly more expensive. Let me explain. Truth exists as energy, as reality, within us. It is not something just in our minds but held within our bodies. In each and every cell of our being. When I tell the truth, I don't have to think about it because the truth lives in my mind and throughout my body. I don't have to remember the truth; it's within me. I cannot lose it.

I

I never thought of truth living in my body. How does that work? And another question: how can being polite by telling someone that I am fine, be expensive?

SAGE

The body remembers our experiences. All of them. So, when I think about the call I got last month from an old friend, my face lights up. I smile because my body remembers the pleasant connection. Another example. My stomach tightens when I drive across the bridge where I had my first car accident. Again, my body remembers. It knows my truth!

To answer your second question, lying is expensive. The first harmful effect of lying is the energy it consumes. First, we must create the lie; then remember the lie. Because the lie is foreign to us, it is not natural. Neither the body nor the mind will acknowledge it because it is not truth. So, it must be actively remembered. And all that takes laborious effort. Telling the truth is much easier!

I

I don't know about that! I think sometimes it is easier to minimize the truth.

SAGE

That's because lying often becomes habitual for us. And if we lie in small things, we will lie in bigger things. My point is: truth is important. So, instead of saying "I'm fine", you could have said "I'm hanging in there" or "life is challenging today" or "I'm just okay" or "I'm struggling a bit." Then if the person asks you for details, you have the option of revealing more or setting a boundary. And you would have been honest with both the person and yourself.

THE SECOND WHY:
THE LAYERS OF ILLUSIONS

SAGE
So why does your energy not match your words? What's really going on today?

I
I guess I'm just conflicted. Everything on the outside is going fine: work, home. But inside, I am all over the place. Mostly I feel muddled. My thoughts and my emotions are all jumbled.

SAGE
Why?

I
I don't know. I haven't thought about it. In fact, I have been trying to stay busy so I wouldn't have to think about it. And you don't have to tell me: I know that is not healthy. But there it is!

SAGE
So, let's approach this from a different angle. I have a question about your relationship. You said two things that seem contradictory. First, I heard you say the break-up was amicable. Then, I heard you say that your partner complained about you frequently. "Harping" and "war zone" were the words I think you used.

Now, both could be true. One could have a volatile relationship and then experience a cordial ending to that partnership. But in my experience, a war zone does not usually transition into a friendly break-up. So, are you lying to me about the true nature of your relationship? Or are you lying to yourself?

I

Wow!!! I can't believe you! Nothing gets past you!! Okay. Well. Since we are talking about truth, I guess I was lying to both of us. Deep down, I am acutely aware of the difficulties in our relationship. The beginning was fantastic; the middle was horrific; and the ending was a "Cold War." It felt like we were enemies, withdrawing from the war in silent bitterness. And Pat was the bitterness; I was the silence. Pat was so angry with me, it felt like she not only didn't love me anymore, she didn't even like me. I felt so beaten down by her criticism and harshness that I couldn't do anything right. Rejected at every turn. When we split, it is just easier to tell people the split was amicable. Maybe because by then, I was so relieved to be done.

SAGE

Another far-reaching effect of lying is that we take a step away from reality. Might be a tiny step but a step none-the-less. Lies are illusions masquerading as the truth. And we are trying to convince others and ourselves the illusions are true. But illusions are not true. Nor are they real. The more we repeat the lie, the more we conceal our truth with illusion, the more difficult it is to own our truth and our reality.

The journey away from our True Self starts with a lie. It continues with more lies until we believe the illusion we have fabricated. Then we start to live the lies and the illusions as if they are facts. And that, my friend, is when we have lost ourselves.

That is why you feel so muddled. You are caught between your lies and your truth. Between your illusions and your reality. And in the long run, truth and reality are always the healthier choice. The adult choice.

TRUTH DEMANDS EXPOSURE

I
But it is so hard to face the truth. Sometimes, I want to; but then I get so terrified. And I don't even know why I'm so terrified. I just am!

SAGE
Isn't that the case! For all of us! The truth can feel daunting and overwhelming. But it is worth the effort of facing our fears.

Truth demands exposure. It begs for us to admit it, to own it. And when we don't, the truth finds all sorts of creative methods to get our attention. Like your face just now not matching your truth. Your body revealed that you are living a disconnect.

When I was an active alcoholic, I lied all the time. Lied about the severity of my addiction. Stole stuff then lied about stealing stuff. Broke commitments then lied about who was to blame. Lied to everyone about my pain. Which was why I was drinking in the first place.

The truth tried many avenues to be seen and heard. My pain kept me awake at night, so I drank to sleep. Then I didn't want to face the day so I drank to get up in the morning. During any down time, my truth would try to speak to me, so I drank whenever I wasn't working. Then people at work would remind me of my pain so I drank at work. By refusing to face my truth, I became a spiraling, hopeless addict.

Then I hit bottom. And the truth could no longer be denied. Got a DUI. Lost my job. Lost my family. Lost my friends. Lost my car. Lost my home. And if all that didn't make it obvious, lost every ounce of self-respect.

The truth seeks exposure. Demands exposure. Because truth is the path to salvation.

THE THIRD WHY
MOTIVE

SAGE

The next step is to examine our motives for lying. So, why did you lie about the ending of your relationship? What was your motive for telling me it was amicable?

I

I'm not sure. Right after we split, when people asked me about the break-up, I just froze. I wasn't sure what to say. Or how much to say. So, I just started saying the split was amicable. They were happy. After all, no one wants to hear the gory details of a bad ending. I was happy because I didn't have to divulge the ugly failures of the relationship. I didn't have to explain anything. But I see your point. I did create an illusion and I have been trying to believe it ever since!

SAGE

Truth is very difficult for us humans. We all struggle with being truthful and honest. Why? Fear! We are afraid of the truth. Telling the truth feels too revealing. We are afraid of being too vulnerable. So, we lie.   What truth were you afraid of?

I

I guess I was afraid Pat was right: That I really was the failure that she thought I was. I felt her disdain and disappointment in me every time she looked at me. If I could believe, or have other people believe, that our break-up was amicable, then at least I could feel better about myself. I wanted to believe that I was not the loser she thought I was. Not the loser I believe I am.

THE FOURTH WHY: LITTLE KIDS IN CHARGE

SAGE
Why did you believe her?

I
I guess because she was so forceful. She took charge and I let her. In the beginning, we talked about everything. But over time, she started to make decisions without consulting me. Here's an example. In deciding to buy new carpeting, we agreed on a color, a maximum price, and that we would lay it ourselves. So, what does she do? She announces one day that she picked out the carpeting and is having it installed the next week. And it cost twice as much as we decided!!

That kind of crap became the norm. She just did what she wanted with no regard for me or my opinion. And I had no power in the relationship. Most of the time, I felt like her butler rather than her partner.

SAGE
Why did your feel powerless?

I
I told you! She just ran over me.

SAGE
So, you sacrificed your self-respect for Pat's opinions? That sounds like one of your little kids inside was in charge. Believe me! I understand that dance! I let my first partner dictate to me so much that my adult self was permanently MIA! It took me a long time to learn to stand in my own power and speak my truth.

THE PRIORITY OF INTEGRITY

SAGE

Although some of my lies were verbal, I was an expert at lying through silence. Whenever we do not speak our truth, we are lying. One of the far-reaching consequences of my lying, especially through silence, was the loss of integrity.

My dance looked like this. I would set a boundary and my partner would crash right through it. I would react one of two ways: occasionally, I would start bullying and berating. More often, I would sulk in steely silence, furious I was getting run over. Neither option was healthy but those were the only two I knew.

Then I started to unpack the messages I was sending myself. And they were quite disturbing. The essence was this: In times of disagreement when I bullied or berated another, I believed my voice was superior to everyone else's. In times of disagreement when I remained silent, I believed my truth should yield to another's. Both, being a bully or being a doormat, were reactions of my kids. Usually, my two-year old bullies; my four-year-old pouts. It took me a while to realize there were more than just those two options.

Because there is a third option! Acting as an adult, I can speak my truth! I can speak my truth with tact and respect. And I can ask that the other person do the same.

Both parties can respectfully speak their truth. Then the next step is to see if we agree, where we disagree, where we can negotiate. This took much practice because I was so afraid. But I made the commitment to stop my part of the dance. If the other person did not choose to respectfully speak the truth, then I could set boundaries to protect myself. Or make other decisions regarding the relationship. And the practice was worth the effort because it is the road to integrity. I learned three crucial lessons.

One. My most valuable asset is integrity. One can sacrifice it, but integrity can never be taken. I gave away my integrity every time I sacrificed my voice for another. Every time I put my truth second to someone else's. Every time my created illusions were valued over reality.

Second. Disagreement is healthy. And we don't have to agree. You don't have to believe a word I say. What we need to do as adults is to respectfully listen to another's truth and speak our own. I may not like your truth or even believe it but I must listen to it. Because that is the only way healthy dialogue happens. And healthy dialogue is essential because that's the only way we learn.

Third. My truth is not more important than another's but it must be my priority. I know my truth because it resides within my body and mind and soul. I must trust it. My truth is more important than fear. More important than looking good to others. More important than making someone else happy. To have integrity and maintain integrity, it must be my priority.

INTO THE WORDS

SAGE

Our choice of words is incredibly important because words are the vehicles to truth. What you say and how you say it matter. Here are some pointers.

I think this is the most crucial one. Always, always use "I" language. Using your carpet fiasco as an example, people often throw blame around by saying: "You screwed up. You were wrong." A healthier way to respond would have been: I am very angry because I was not consulted when our agreement changed."

Blame almost always escalates the tension because it almost always leads to defensiveness and then a counter attack. "I" language honestly owns what one feels with little room for the other person to refute.

The human brain struggles to understand the word "not." When I say, "I am not angry" my brain slides right over the "not" to believe I am angry. So rather than state the negative, speak in the positive. "I feel confused" "or "I feel ambivalent."

We also have trouble with the word "can't." My energy freezes when I say, "I can't do this" and I remain stuck. So, the very least, say "I can't do this yet." Even better is saying, I will work on learning this."

So, language is important. And what I say to myself is most important! Practice. And keep practicing. Then practice some more. Remember to seek progress not perfection![20]

---

[20] AA.

THE FIFTH WHY:
THE DEEP TRUTH

SAGE
So, why did you remain powerless with Pat? You had options. You could have talked to her. Told Pat how you felt. You could have gone to therapy. Either alone or together. Solo therapy might have helped give you some tools to dealing with Pat. You chose to stay in the war zone. Why did you stay?

Now I want you to dig deep. Very deep. And this might be incredibly painful to uncover. But it needs to be unearthed and explored and owned. Why did you not stand up to Pat? Why did you remain in victimhood?

I
I never thought of this before; I never connected the dots. I guess, I felt like I deserved it. I was the victim with Pat because I have always been the victim. And you are absolutely right: this is very difficult. Difficult to remember. Difficult to admit.

SAGE
Who taught you to be the victim?

I
My father, I guess. When I was young, I idolized him. Thought he was the greatest man on earth. My fondest memories of him were when he walked me home from school. He would ask me about my day, what I had for lunch, who I played with at recess. I was so proud of holding his hand, telling my friends he was my dad.

As I got older, he got more distant, more remote. I tried and tried everything I could think of to win his love. I would follow him around, bring him his morning coffee, ask questions about soccer because he was a fan. I even played soccer as a kid to make him proud of me. But to no avail. No matter what I did, it felt like he no longer liked me. Or wanted me. And I thought it was all my fault. I must have done something to drive him away.

SAGE
That must have hurt a great deal. I am so sorry that was your experience with your father. It sounds like when you were very young the relationship was good. But then it shifted. What about after the divorce? Did you see him much after your parents split up?

I
After the divorce, I seldom saw him. He would say he wanted to see me but then call to cancel. That solidified my belief that he didn't love or want me. I missed him so much but after some time, I quit wanting him. It hurt too much. And I knew I would never have him in my life. So quitting was better than hoping.

SAGE
How did your parents make decisions? Like buying new carpet?

I
If my parents were getting new carpet, my mom would ask my dad what he wanted and he would say the same thing each time: I don't care. So, she just got whatever she wanted.

SAGE
Our issues always repeat themselves. The people or circumstances may change a bit; but the issues remain. Glaring at us to recognize them. Are you able to see some of your patterns? But before we connect the dots

75

of your relationships, I want to quote the Buddhist teacher, Pema Chodron. She reminds us that, in reviewing our behavior, the first step is to just observe. Yes, you will have to deal with the emotional fall-out but first, just be an observer of your history. Reflect on your past without emotion. Just observe what happened. That's the first step when unpacking history. Okay?

I

I guess so. This sounds like it's going to hurt!

SAGE

Probably. But the only way is through. You have tried denial and running away. Now is the time for facing the truth. For healing. So. Here are a few connections I observe in listening to your story.

One. Both relationships start out positive only to end in bitter loss. Your dad leaves. Pat leaves.

Two. Both break agreements with you without discussion. Your dad in making plans with you; Pat in buying carpet. Now the carpet might be an isolated event, but I doubt it. If you reflect on your partnership, I would wager there is a pattern of you both making an agreement, and then Pat breaking it. And for the record, Pat is not to blame. You both did the dance. You both hold responsibility for that dance. And its aftermath.

Three. As a child, you didn't have the skills to articulate your needs or stand up for yourself. You didn't know how to let your dad know how much pain you were in when he wasn't around. Now for a shocker! That child was often the one in relationship with Pat. Still unable - - because your child was in charge – to get your needs met. To be fair, your kids were not always in charge. But during disagreements, your kids took control. This happens for most of us. Out of desperation because we do not know how to be an adult.

Four. You keep repeating the same behavior hoping for a different outcome. Einstein called this the definition of insanity. And we all do it. We keep doing the same thing hoping to get the solution we want. But it never happens. You kept trying to win both your father's love and Pat's respect. But all that trying did not make them love you. Or make them respect you. Or make them stay.

Five. You are caught in a vicious cycle that is common to most of us if we are honest. Because you feel powerless and don't admit it, you remain a victim. Because you feel like a victim and don't face it, you remain powerless.

Six. You try and try but when your efforts fail, you quit. At least emotionally. You want to believe that quitting will ease the pain. Quitting does stop future pain. But the pain you already have incurred remains. And that pain and grief must be faced. No matter who leaves.

Seven. In the end, both your dad and your partner leave you. And you feel at fault. You are left believing that you are totally to blame for what others do. Believing that no one wants you. Believing that you are, indeed, a loser. An unlovable loser.

I
I never saw that! All those patterns!

SAGE
This is a common element in our lives. We repeat patterns over and over until we recognize them and learn their lessons. That is the way we heal.

THE ESSENCE OF WHY

I

I never saw ll those connections. I had no idea I all that stuff was there. All that stuff about my dad. About Pat. All that stuff about me.

SAGE

If you noticed, I asked you "why?" five different times. We all bury stuff. Stuff we are afraid of. Shame. Guilt. Grief. We bury our loss. Our pain. Our lost dreams. Our unrealized hope. Thinking that burying it will make all our issues magically disappear. Burying doesn't fix anything. Burying doesn't heal anything. Our issues just wait for us to retrieve them. To heal them. So, one must dig and dig and dig to unbury them from their graves of denial.

Here's an important truth. Every time, you get bothered by someone or something, it's about you. Every time. You get cut off in traffic, it's about you. Your boss schedules you on a day you thought you had off, it's about you. Your partner ignores you, it's about you. Now, you are not the center of the world. But everything is about you. Everything that happens is pushing your buttons to see if you are ready to dig and dig and dig out your stuff. Ready to dig out the truth.

I was taught to ask myself five whys.[21] So, you ask yourself "why?" Again and again and again and again and again. Because each time, as you dig a little deeper, you will get a little closer to the truth. And a little more of yourself back from the grave.

---

[21] Connor Blacksher, conversation with author, January, 2023.

CIRCLING BACK: EVERYTHING IS CONNECTED

SAGE

So, let's circle back to lying. I think we lie for one of two reasons: to avoid punishment or to gain a reward. You lied about the ending of your relationship to gain the reward of feeling good about yourself. Most of the lies I told were to avoid punishment. But no matter what the reason, results were the same. We lie. And it costs us. A lot!

So, now let me tell you why lies are so expensive. Denying our truth, the truth that lies within us, denies our integrity. Takes away our self-respect. When I lie, I know, at my core, I am running away from myself. I am letting fear dictate my behavior. In the moment, I can always rationalize the lie. But it will always leave me feeling hollow. And not liking who I am.

When I start to believe the lies that I tell myself as well as the lies others tell me, again, I lose myself. A great example. Are you a loser because your father left? Absolutely not! You were a child wanting and needing to be loved. Are you a loser because Pat left you? Again, absolutely not. Having a broken relationship doesn't make you a loser. It makes you human.

Your job now is to be honest with yourself about the lessons within those relationships. The commitment to honesty is much more than escaping punishment or getting rewarded. It's choosing self-respect. It's valuing integrity above everything else.

When you have integrity and self-respect, you know you are choosing yourself. And that is most important.

TRUTH WITH DISCRETION

I
So, I should always speak the truth?

SAGE
When I am an adult, I need to always, always, speak the truth to myself. When I was a child, I sometimes had to lie to myself to survive. As an adult, I face my truth, no matter what it is.

Telling the truth to others requires more discretion. I need to speak the truth to others "except when to do so would injure them or others."[22] To understand this, I will set forth three levels for us to ponder. First, the less consequential. For example, your partner says, "Do I look good in the dress?" Or your boss asks if you like the new corporate policy. Be truthful with diplomacy. Tact and sensitivity can answer questions like these honestly without harshness or cruelty or risk.

The second is speaking my truth even if it hurts another. Notice I said "hurts" but not "injures." Subtle but big difference. Examples where I must speak the truth. Telling my partner, I no longer want to be in relationship. Telling my kids that I lost my job because of my alcoholism instead of blaming it on an economic downturn. Telling a friend that I will not cover for her stealing from the company.

Situations like this may hurt another, cause them pain or grief but speaking the truth is vital. Lying would just be denial. An important spiritual tenet is this: when I move toward my own spiritual health, it always opens the door for another to do the same. So, when I tell my partner I am done with our relationship, it will cause

---

[22] Step Nine of AA.

hurt. But it will also open the door for my partner to examine her part of the dance. Her attitude and behaviors that contributed to our break-up. She may not want to do that but the door is open none-the-less for her to see her own reality.

I

I get that. But when do you not speak the truth?

SAGE

"Injuring others" refers to causing serious harm that one does not need to cause. For example, I need to confront my partner if I think he has a drug problem, speaking my truth about how I been affected by his using. That might hurt him but it is imperative I speak my truth and not sugar-coat my reality. But I have no business calling his boss to report my partner's absence from work because he was high. The result may be his firing and that's injuring him unnecessarily. And it is not my place to report him to his boss.

Another example, discretion is necessary when dealing with folks with developmental issues or dementia. If an elder with Alzheimer's does not remember her son died, repeating it so that elder must mourn that loss again is causing unnecessary injury.

Using discretion demands two considerations. First, is it my story to tell? If Mom wants to share something private about Dad with the kids, it is not the Mom's story to tell. Second, will it cause injury? Telling this private thing about Dad may damage his relationship with his children. Thereby causing injury. So, on both counts, mom must remain silent.

TRUTH WITH HUMOR

SAGE

Let me tell you a story where I found humor in speaking the truth. Having a product question that could only be answered by an agent, I got stuck in the automated customer service loop. For the third time, I tried to talk to a live person.

But no.

The irritatingly calm automated voice kept saying: "In order to get you to the right person, I will need more information."

The first time I called and got stuck in the loop the voice told me that my issue could be handled via the automated email.

It could not.

The second time I called and asked, politely I might add, for a representative, I got connected to automated billing.

Which I did not need.

Or want.

So, the third time I called and the voice once again said, "I need more information." I said, "I am very frustrated by your automated system. and I want to talk to someone about it!"

I got a live person immediately.

THE TRUTHS I TELL MYSELF

I am an adult with little kids inside whom I parent.

I act with integrity.

I speak my truth with clarity and tact.

I refuse to be stuck on the dualism
        of being a bully or being a doormat.
 I stand in my power to speak my truth.

I can and will set healthy boundaries
        whenever others disrespect me.

I let go of my anger, resentment, blame, and self-pity
        and embrace the porcupine of truth.

I commit to truth and integrity is my priority.

I speak my truth
        and let go of the outcome.

ILLUSION & WISDOM

THE ILLUSION OF THE RIGHT CHOICE

I
I need to talk about my cousin. We had lunch together the other day and I just don't understand the choices he's making. He is a senior at the University of MN and he wants to quit! Can you believe it?! He wants to drop out of college! With less than one year to go, he wants to quit! I told him he wasn't thinking this through. He just kept telling me that his choices were the right ones for him. But they aren't!

SAGE
Perhaps he is on a different path than the one you took.

I
I don't care what path he is on. It's the wrong one. He is making a gigantic mistake!

SAGE
Each person has a path to walk. Lessons to learn. Your cousin has his own path to walk. Even if you don't agree with it. Perhaps it is the best path for him.

I
No! This decision of his is not the right one!

SAGE
Why? Because he is not taking the path you took? Because he is not taking the path you want him to take? What makes you so sure you know what he should do with his life? Are you omnipotent?

I
No. Of course not. But I do know that quitting college now is ridiculous.

SAGE
Why is that ridiculous?

I
He will have a mountain of debt and nothing to show for it. He needs to finish. A degree makes a huge difference. That's just common sense!

SAGE
Maybe it's not about logic. Why can't you support your cousin's decision? Even if you disagree with it?

I
Because his decision is not a wise one. He is making a huge mistake and he doesn't see it!

SAGE
Even if that is true, and I don't believe it is, why can't you support him?

I
Because he is wrong! Why are you being so adversarial?

SAGE
Why are you so invested in your cousin doing life your way? Are you his Higher Power? Are you God?

I
Now you are just being preposterous!!

SAGE
I don't think so. I think you are very vested in him making the decision that you think is best. There are two issues here and they are both yours. Not your cousin's. Are you willing to look at them?

I
We can look but I know I am right. I have been where he is and finishing college is the right choice.

SAGE
First issue. I don't know if your way is the best decision for him and neither do you. Finishing college was the best choice for <u>you</u> in walking <u>your</u> path. But that doesn't mean it is his best choice. Look, there are many paths to take in life. One school of philosophy proposes that each person must walk each and every path possible. So, in one life, you finished college. But you had a life when you did not even go to college. A life when you started and quit. A life when you succeeded in college. A life where you failed. You experienced every possible scenario to learn every possible lesson.

My point is you don't know which path he is on or which lessons he is trying to learn this lifetime. He will figure out if he made the best decision in his own way. In the meantime, you support him. If he asks for advice, and only if he asks, then you share your experience with him. You don't preach or pontificate or dictate. You simply share your experience. Then you go back to supporting him in his decision. Whatever that might be.

I

Even if it leads to a lifetime of heartache? Even if it's the dumbest decision ever?

SAGE

Yes. Because you don't know that it is the dumbest decision ever. You don't know what he is trying to learn. You can only make the decision for your path. He needs to make the decisions for his. Then he can learn the lessons that present themselves. Your job is to support him. Without judgement or ridicule. Make sense?

I

Well no. What if he wants to go out and kill someone? What if he wants to chase someone down after getting cut off in traffic and beat that person. Do I support him in that?

SAGE

Now who's being preposterous? The short answer is: you don't support his behavior; you support him. There is a difference between encouraging an action and supporting the person. I never want to embolden someone's actions that may inflict harm.

In your scenario, I would not tell him what to do. From my own experience, if you try to tell me what to do, I would either do the opposite just out of spite or turn my wrath on you. So, I might ask him, "Could we sit down for a minute so you can tell me why you are so angry?" Or I might say, "The last time I got so angry at a driver, it helped to take some deep breaths before I did anything."

But I cannot control what he does. If he beats someone up, I don't support his decision. But I do stand by him and support him in learning the lessons of a criminal assault and the aftermath that will result from that decision. See the difference?

I

I guess. I just feel I have answers that will help my cousin. I don't want him to make useless mistakes.

SAGE

And my point is that no mistake is useless. All hold a lesson we need to learn. You job is learn yours and walk with him as he learns his. It's easy and fun to think we know best. But you don't know what is best for him. You only know what is best for you. And that, my friend, is enough of a job!

Second issue. Why is it so important that he follow your path? I am trying to get you to see that you may not know what is best for him. And to look at why you are so invested in his choices. His decision really doesn't affect you at all. So why are you so invested? So angry with him? So pushy? So adamant?

I

Because I am right.

SAGE

Wanting to be "right" and thinking we are "right" are dangerous attitudes. The only person —and I mean the ONLY person— I may be "right" about is me. And even that is a crapshoot. Look. I gather information regarding a decision, then I make the best choice for me at that point in time. Sometimes, that decision is great; sometimes, it is tolerable; sometimes it is downright disastrous. My job is to learn the lessons the situation presents. If I don't, I will just keep making the same mistakes until I do. There is no escape from my lessons.

I believe that when I get invested in being "right" about other folks, there are usually two fear-based issues in play. One. I want to be important. My ego takes control and I want to play God. I think I know what is best for others. I believe I am smarter than others. I can solve their problems because I know their answers.

Playing God is an extremely dangerous illusion. One that I have played many times. The reality is that I barely know what is best for me, let alone what is best for another. Playing God is always an illusion of control. Of importance. Of power. If I look deeper, playing God just exposes my fears of being vulnerable and powerless.

I

I don't get that. I don't see vulnerability in this at all! What vulnerabilities?

SAGE

That brings me to the second fear-based issue. Humans have a deep-seated dread of being wrong. We ask ourselves: What if I make the wrong decision? What if I make a mistake? Deep down, I fear my errors will separate me from others. Isolate me. Condemn me. And that fear is the fear of vulnerability.

But if others make the same choice I did, then I feel better. I tell myself that if two of us made the same decision, then it must be the right one. And the more people who make that decision, the more "right" I must be. Furthermore, even if I am incorrect, I won't be alone. So, I won't feel isolated.

That is why conformity is so alluring. Conformity weaves the illusion that all of us can't be wrong! We seek comfort and security within the group. Which makes it harder for us to walk our own path.

I

I agree with that! It is scary to decide against the crowd. I do feel that there is safety in numbers. Like you said: if everyone in my group is thinking the same way, we can't all be wrong! And to be honest, I do feel important when I give advice that I think is right! So, I guess my ego is involved. Maybe more than a bit!! So, what's the bottom line?

SAGE

Let go of the illusion that there is a "right" answer for another and you know what it is. In fact, let go of "right" and "wrong" altogether. Instead, search for the lessons in your own life. Know that they are hidden in plain sight in every situation you encounter.

Commit to walking your path and commit to walking beside others on theirs. Put all your effort into making decisions that keep you on your path, while resisting the temptation to tell others what to do. When you do slip into that, recognize you are playing God. That your ego is in control.

See conformity for what it is: an illusion. It doesn't matter if everyone agrees with you or no one agrees with you. You walk your path. Face the fear of walking your path alone if need be.

Remember this paradox. You are not the center for the world and everything is about you. Everything is a lesson for you. Make the best possible decisions at this moment in time for yourself. Then let go of the outcome.

THE PORCUPINE OF ILLUSION

I

The fact that I have illusions is new to me. Would you explain more about illusions?

SAGE

Absolutely! Everybody has illusions. Only the wise realize this. And only the wisest dispel their illusions and embrace awareness and reality.

Illusions are misleading or false perceptions of reality. Misinterpretations of our insights or senses. A piece of information comes to us but we don't want to face it. So, usually unconsciously, we take a side-step from the truth. We deny the reality of our information. And we create an illusion.

I

Why do that? Why not just face reality?

SAGE

We get scared because reality can be very challenging. Overwhelming. Painful. So, we create illusions to help us avoid reality until we are ready to face it. Problem is, the illusions become so ingrained within us, we forget that they're illusions we created to cope with life. We begin to believe the illusions are real.

I

Examples, please?

SAGE

Of course. As a child, I shaped the illusion that my parents were loving. Often, illusions are a child's best route of survival. No kid can take in, let alone process, the reality that mom or dad are, in fact, mean or cruel.

So, I created the illusion that I had good parents. That led to another illusions: If they hurt me, it was because I deserved it. So, I ended up blaming myself for my own mistreatment! It took a long time to untangle the illusion and see the reality that my parents were abusive. And they were totally responsible for the abuse. Not me.

Another example. For a long time, I believed I had a deep relationship with one of my friends. Even though I was the only one reaching out. Even after I did not get an invitation to her wedding. I still bought into my illusion that we were close and refused to accept reality. Because I wanted this relationship so desperately, I manufactured one. And of course, a manufactured relationship is not a real one. For whatever reason, the friendship was one-sided. I was the only one asking for connection; I was the only one making all the contacts. When I finally could see the disparity, I could see the illusion and then, I could quit chasing her.

Another example. I worked for a toxic institution for decades, fashioning the illusion that the abusive institution was acting in my best interests. Until I woke up to the reality that the institution was only protecting itself.

I

You are always talking about fear as a motivator. I bet fear is involved in our creation of illusions.

SAGE

Yes. Most illusions are created out of a "reward-punishment" dichotomy. We seek a real or perceived prize; we fear a real or perceived retribution. Here are some more examples.

I stayed in a relationship long after it was over because I was afraid to leave, afraid I'd be alone. So, to stay, I crafted a very common illusion: things will change. The relationship would get better, my partner will want to connect with me, everything would magically work out for us. Despite all the evidence to the contrary, I bought the illusion. Eventually, I saw reality: nothing got better, nothing changed. The relationship ended and I moved on despite my fears.

I have a friend who bought into the illusion of pursuing a career for money, thinking it would make him happy. After twelve years, he was miserable, worn out, depressed, bitter, and resentful. The illusion of financial reward was killing him!

Another example. And this is a huge illusion! It's the belief that someone else knows what we need to do. Someone more educated or more experienced has the answers that we don't have. Like a doctor or a therapist or a minister or a teacher. We want someone to tell us our own answers. The reality is each of us has all the answers we need. We know our truth and we know what to do.

That does not mean we don't need help. Fear can paralyze us and we forget that we have our own answers. So, gather information. Talk to others and ask questions. Heed their experience. Then, listen to yourself. And trust yourself to make the best decision for yourself at that point in time.

Related to that is the illusion that a bigger entity like cultural norms or societal standards or religious dogmas holds the answer for us. I know many folks refusing to leave dysfunctional relationships because the church says "no" to divorce or because society says you can't leave your kids. Fear again traps us in the illusion that church or culture is "right." Truth is, I also know many folks who got divorced and thrived. And the kids thrived. And the ex-spouse had the opportunity to thrive. You don't have to follow norms that don't fit. You know what your truth is and what your reality is. And you can create new norms. Ones that match your truth and reality.

I

I think I know another illusion that is common. A fellow teacher at my school weighs about 325 pounds. Because of hip and knee issues, he wants to have a hip replacement but none of the three doctors he has seen will approve it until he loses some weight. This teacher just keeps going to another specialist in hopes that one will do the surgery. That's an illusion, right? The illusion that a hip replacement will fix everything?

SAGE

Yes. He has a root issue he does not want to face. So, he used food to escape. Now, his illusion is that hip surgery will fix the effects of his eating disorder, which he used to ignore the root problem. Until he faces his real issue and deals with it, a new hip won't help.

I

I bet I too have a lot of illusions to face. Any advice for how to do that?

SAGE

As always, be gentle. We all have illusions. They may have served us once so the question to ask is: does this illusion serve me now? Or am I willing to see reality?

Illusions are a state of being deceived. Other people can betray us with their illusions. And I need to deal with that appropriately. But the illusions I need to focus on are mine. The places I deceive myself. Work to uncover my illusions without harsh judgment. Seek awareness of the lessons behind the illusions.

"WE ALL DO BETTER WHEN WE ALL DO BETTER"[23]

I
Wait! Won't others be adversely affected if we dismantle our illusions?

SAGE
My movement toward wholeness can never lead another from wholeness. She or he may choose to stay unhealthy, but that is their decision. I can only choose to be real and healthy for myself.

Let me share the common illusion of being a good parent with you. Popular and as old as time! Mom and Dad want to give little James everything. So, growing up James didn't have to do chores like doing the dishes or cleaning his room. In adolescence, James didn't have to get a job or make his own money. Even in adulthood, when James had a good job, Mom and Dad paid for many of his basics, like car insurance. Thus, James never learned to be financially responsible. Then at 38, James fell on economic hard times. But he had no clue how to weather the storm.

Mom and Dad held the illusion that by giving James financial support, they were good parents. But they failed to give him what he needed most: lessons in responsibility, self-reliance, interdependence. If they would have embraced the reality that good parenting is teaching children financial accountability, James would have been much better equipped to be an adult.

Mom and Dad dispelling their illusions would not adversely affect James. In fact, the opposite. James would have valuable financial lessons that would serve him throughout his life.

---

[23] Paul Wellstone.

COMMITMENT TO AWARENESS

I

I know you said the motive for our illusions is usually because reality is too hard to face. So, we side-step it. How do we avoid that?

SAGE

It starts with a commitment to honesty. Remember a while back, we talked about your facial expression not matching what you were feeling? That's a good example of small lies starting to create illusions.

Sometimes I don't want to admit my feelings, even to myself. So, I use words that hide the power and reality of my true feelings. I am not furious I tell myself; I am only a little miffed. I'm not depressed, just a just down. These little side-steps from the truth are illusions that become destructive as I start to believe what I say rather than the reality of what I feel.

The reality is I feel what I feel. Emotions are just that: emotions. They rise like waves on the ocean. I don't have to act on them but I do need to name them. Naming my emotions reveals my reality. Then I can decide what I need to do with those emotions. But if I deny their identity, I deny their existence. And they will always return. And the waves will be bigger!

So, I commit to being aware of my truth. To accurately naming exactly what I feel, when I feel it. To that end, I love synonyms. The bigger my vocabulary, the better for naming my reality.

Anger can be fury, rage, quarrelsomeness, belligerence, vindictiveness, sulking, aggression, bitterness, resentment, passive aggression, bullying, antagonistic, confrontational.

Greed includes hoarding, grasping, clutching, envy, pride, jealousy, vanity, wanting, craving, conceit, self-centeredness, addiction.

Pain is sadness, hurt, agony, grief, aching....

I

Okay! I get it. You can stop being a thesaurus.

SAGE

The next step in avoiding side-stepping reality is a commitment to awareness. Awareness that we have illusions and don't even know it! This is hard to admit because we all like to think we are omnipotent. Admitting we deceive ourselves makes us feel dumb and inadequate and that makes us feel vulnerable. But we are not omnipotent. We are humans who create illusions to deal with the harshness of life. And then, if we are wise, we dismantle our illusions to embrace our reality.

This demand integrating our past and our present, our successes and our regrets. The fundamental question is always — always — am I willing to learn? Everything holds a lesson. And we all have much to learn. That fact does not make us dumb. It makes us human. And the only foolishness in life is when I refuse to learn the lessons presented. Luckily, my Higher Power gives me multiple opportunities to move past my resistance!

I

I get that. And I admit I probably have a bunch of illusions. But I don't think they have influenced my life as much as you think they do. I am doing pretty well in my life right now.

SAGE

I beg to differ! When you first came to me, you said you were lost and your life was falling apart. So — what did I say just now that scared you?

THE GREATEST ILLUSION

I

I guess it was that part about integrating my past and my present. I don't really want to look back at my childhood. It's too painful. I don't suppose there is another way? Just heal my present and forget the past?

SAGE

This is the greatest illusion of all: that denying the past will not affect the present. It does. Always!

Here's an example. A woman knows that when she was ten, she was sexually abused by her uncle. But she thinks that the past will not affect her present. After all, she has remembered the abuse. She knows it happened. She wants to believe that the sexual damage done to her will magically go away. Her illusion is that remembering is enough.

Remembering is not enough, just the first step. So, at forty years of age, married with kids, she is emotionally distant and sexually frozen. She has built huge walls so not one gets close. Does not like sex, certainly doesn't enjoy it. Just longs for it to be over.

The past will always impact the present and compartmentalizing it is ultimately an expensive and ineffective effort to avoid healing. Bottom line: all our wounds demand to be healed by feeling the pain, not just remembering it, in order to release it.

Healing is the path to freedom from suffering. Integrating the past is the only way to live a healthy present and have a hopeful future.

I

So, what do I do?

ONE DECISION

SAGE

Realize that "we are all one decision away from calamity."[24] I know, it sounds too dramatic. But it is true. Certainly, in the physical world. Do I steal that money when no one is looking? Do I cheat on my partner when I am a continent away? Do I throw away five years of sobriety because my boss yelled at me? All examples of one decision away from calamity.

But it is also true in the emotional realm. Do I refuse to integrate because I am afraid? Do I continue to be miserable rather than face myself and my truth? Do I move forward to continue to spin in circles? Again. All examples of one decision away from calamity.

Let me give you an example from Overeaters Anonymous. "It's not eating one greener bean that will get you in trouble. It's the decision to eat one green bean." That decision leads to a slippery slope where I start to justify all sorts of movements away from integrity and honesty and awareness and healing.

You see, it's the decision that is important. Not the outcome. Spiritual progress is measured by our decisions to make the effort. So, even if I can only take the smallest of steps today, that is what I want and need my decision to be. Always toward healing. Always toward my True Self.

P.J. Tracy, *Ice Cold Killer*, Crooked Lane Books, New York City, NY, 2019, 49.

CHOOSE WISELY

I

That sounds incredibly difficult. And scary. And painful.

SAGE

Yes. But the alternative is worse. To remain in fear and pain. To live an unlived life. To be stuck in the lie of illusions. Living in illusion is a choice we make. Living in reality is a choice we make. So here are some questions you need to ask yourself and answer honestly, remembering willingness is the key.[25] Not perfection.

Do I really want to know myself?

Will I let in the reality that I am courageous and strong? Or settle for the illusion that fear will defeat me?

Will I make the decision to move forward
Or remain scared and in pain?

Here's a fact: you will stay where you are until you decide you don't have to stay there anymore. So perhaps the real question is:
Are you tired of being miserable?

---

[25] AA motto.

THE GIFT OF REALITY

I

I often want to forget how miserable I feel. Once the misery is passed and I feel better, I just want to move on. And hope it doesn't return. But it does. But I wonder if facing myself is worth it? What if I don't feel better? What if facing reality just leads to more misery?

SAGE

Growth is painful! But I believe the results are worth the effort. Because I would rather live in reality than illusion. Rather be real than fake. No matter what the costs.

Because the harrowing challenge of facing myself brings a gift that I cannot buy anywhere — Wisdom.

You can achieve wisdom a couple of ways. You can reflect or meditate or pray, thereby connecting to the Source of Wisdom. A second way you attain wisdom is through experience. Paradoxically, I believe the first method will lead you to the second and the second will lead you to the first. That is because wisdom is the integration of the spiritual world and emotional world.

Rumi, the twelfth century poet mystic, summed it up best. "Yesterday I was clever, so I wanted to change the world. Today I am wise, so I am changing myself."[26]

So, facing myself is worth the pain and effort because it leads to wisdom. And wisdom is the path to Enlightenment.

---

[26] Rumi, https://www.goodreads.com/quotes/tag/wisdom (accessed Sept 12,2023.)

ATTACHMENT & SURRENDER

FUCK YOU GOD

I
How'd you get to be so wise?

SAGE
Believe me, any wisdom I have has been earned through much stimulating experience. Let me explain. A few years ago, I found myself on a new planet. Not an actual planet, of course But a spiritual plane that felt as foreign and alien as a new world. I had no idea where I was or what I was supposed to do.

All I could do is sit on the shoreline eating bark and dirt and rocks. The most exasperating part was that there was a perfectly good pizza right in front of me but I couldn't eat it. Why? I have no idea. But I continued to eat rocks and dirt and bark.

I felt lost and frustrated. After all, I had listened to the Universe; had done everything asked. I earned my doctorate. Then left a very secure teaching position to start my spirituality school. But nothing worked out as I wanted. No one flocked to consult me; only a few signed up for my classes. Despite intense advertising and massive effort, my business did not grow. I had followed my Higher Power and now wanted the fruits of my devotion. But that didn't happen.

I felt professionally, personally, emotionally, and spiritually devastated. I was depressed, angry, lonely, and very resentful. And on top of all that, financially in need of a job. So, I relinquished some of my dreams and went back to the mainstream. After about fifty applications, the only offer I got was at Target.

My pain broke through like a torrent river bursting its dam. Every part of my being hurt. I did not have a rewarding career that sustained me. My life wasn't fulfilling or successful. I was not the guiding teacher I longed to be. And I was living on chocolate and ice cream. If all that weren't enough, I had another eye surgery which resulted in complications. I was completely broken and hit bottom. My rage boiled over at God. And my list of resentments was long. Very long.

Where was God when I was getting raped and beaten as a child? Why didn't I get loving parents? Then I had healed from this horrific childhood, so where was my pay-off? I had four decades of teaching experience, almost four decades of recovery, and written multiple books. So, why isn't my school flourishing? Instead, I was working at Target, pushing carts, putting abandon merchandise back on the shelf. Finally broken, in full despair, I screamed, "Fuck you, God!"

Most of us think this but are afraid to admit it. I was lost, scared, empty, abandoned — at the bottom with two choices before me: stay in despair or surrender. I could stay in self-pity or embrace this new planet as a learning opportunity. Believe me. I stayed in self-pity for a long time. But finally, I tried surrender.

And that is when wisdom arrives. When we surrender. My job was to accept the reality before me and see what it had to teach me. So, I began to become inquisitive about my new challenge. That curiosity deepened my clarity. What I found was that I got nothing that I wanted and everything I needed. Because after stocking shelves, pushing carts, and cleaning up after everyone else in the store —I found a glimmer of Enlightenment at Target.

THE LURE OF ATTACHMENT

I
But you just wanted to be successful. Isn't that normal? Isn't that a healthy thing to desire?

SAGE
It's a human thing to desire but like everything else, desire can easily turn into attachment. And attachment always leads us into trouble.

I
I don't understand. What attachments? And how can my wanting success lead to trouble?

SAGE
Attachment has many personalities. It manifests itself as obsession, control, craving, desire, wanting, lust, hunger, compulsion. And attachment has a ferocious appetite. It consumes us.

Let's be blunt: life is hard. This planet is a beautiful and harsh place. Bad things happen: abuse, cheating, stealing, diseases, illness, plagues, violence, wars, poverty, addictions, ineptness, stupidity! Getting paralyzed by fear, shame, guilt, pain, lies, and illusions, we expected "God" to save us. Then feel abandoned when we are not. We may not say [or even consciously think] "Fuck You God." But our actions shout it. We stop believing. Stop trusting. Stop connecting. We feel abandoned by God so we abandoned God right back. We sink into a self-survivalist mentality, where we don't need a Higher Power — we can do all on our own. Furthermore, we start to believe we don't want "God" because we can be our own god.

That's when our desire quadruples and our attachments seriously injure us. I'll use success as my example. Many folks have made "success" their goal and done everything to achieve it. Compromised values, sacrificed relationships, forfeited integrity. If that weren't sufficient trouble, the successes they have accumulated are never enough.

I

Are you saying the drive for success always leads to trouble? Because I know some folks who are successful and seem to be doing just fine.

SAGE

What I know to be truth for me, is when life does not work out the way I want, I get angry. Which leads me to sink into not trusting my Higher Power and trying to do life on my own. And this plan of isolated survivalism does not work. It will not bring us happiness or peace. But it does allow us to wallow in self-pity and blame.

Success in not a bad thing. It just is. The trouble develops when I want more. The success I have is not enough. I want more. The money and fame that success brings is not enough. I want more. Then success starts to be my god and no matter how successful I am, what I have will never be enough.

For me, the way out of this self-destructive spin was to get angry at "God." I believe the Universe can take all my anger and pain, thus helping me to discover the answers I need. And along the way I learn how to accept life's harshness and embrace life's wonder. I have been able to make peace that I don't get what I want, but I always get what I need.

ATATACHMENT TO FALSE SECURITY

I
Why do we always want more?

SAGE
We are never satisfied with what we have most often because we're afraid of losing what we have. It's really about security. One of our greatest fears is not having security. So, we think more is the answer. If I have more money, I will have financial security. If I have more fame, public adoration will keep me from being lonely. If I have more than you, at least I'm not at the bottom. We think more is the answer. Always more.

The problem is, this type of security is false. Money, prestige, titles —none of this is real security. Authentic security comes from knowing and trusting in a Higher Power. Not in material objects or physiological attributes or having the right partner. This is so difficult for us because it means letting go of societal goals and seeking spiritual ones. Our achievements will not be marked by dollar signs but by accumulation of wisdom.

I
Is it worth it? To let go of success?

SAGE
It is for me. I have always found the glamor of this world lacking. And wanting or craving always — always —ultimately leaves me hollow.

I had let go of society's definition of success and wrote my own. To me, success is being whole. Being real. Being authentic. Most of all, it's liking who I see in the mirror: defects, assets, warts, beauty marks. All of me. Success is accepting myself. Because I am enough.

ATTACHMENT TO CONTROL

I
I had a very hard week. The administration at my school is so stupid. They make these arbitrary decisions that don't help anyone! Not the teachers and certainly not the students. And they don't listen to anyone!

SAGE
I'm sorry work is so challenging. It can be very frustrating when others don't listen or make decisions that make no sense to us. How are you handling it?

I
I'm thinking of quitting.

SAGE
I feel your angst but that seems a bit extreme. Are you willing to step back a moment and look at the big picture? Let's examine this from a different angle. What would happen if everyone did what you wanted?

I
The school would be more student focused. Less bull. Less paperwork. After all, teachers know more about the needs of a classroom than any administrator.

SAGE
It's probably truth that teachers do know more about teaching. But what happens to the direction of the school if everyone did what you wanted them to do? Any downside to your visions? Does the administration know more about some things than you do?

I

Well, I suppose. I don't work with the public. Or with the superintendent's forces. Or even with the parents very much. I get your point: I am looking at things only from my perspective.

SAGE

Yes, I am trying to help you appreciate your issues from another's perspective. That another has problems that you may not even be aware of. Or comprehend. Or want to. That is my first point.

My second point is as you grow in wisdom, you shower others with grace. Yes, grace. Because they are doing the best they can. And they are trying to learn their own tough lessons. Just like you. Remember, this is a learning planet. Everyone, everywhere is working on their own lessons. When I remember that, I am more compassionate. And more patient.

I

I must admit, I have a hard time being patient when others make such stupid decisions!

SAGE

I think that is a hard lesson for everyone on the planet right now. But an important one. Because when I have compassion, I can let go of blame. And that opens me up to get to the heart of the matter: identifying my control. So, in your case, you are trying to control everyone to get what you want. What would happen if you let go?

I

I don't want to let go. I want them to see I know how to make the school better. This is not just about my ego. The administration is always talking about the possibility that we may have to close. Great classrooms could change that!

SAGE
So, you are responsible for not only your classroom's success but your school's survival.

I
Oh, come on! I'm not saying that! I just want to help build a better school. A better place for kids.

SAGE
But before you can focus outside yourself, you need to focus inside yourself. We often do this. We concentrate on the "other." Our family, co-workers, the guy who cut you off in traffic. In your case, you are concentrating on the administration. Believing if you fix them, your problems will be solved. That is an illusion. Because the issues are yours. And fixing the administration will not fix your issues. Or teach you your lessons.

I
After all our time together, I know what you're going to say: I need to look at my past to figure out why I am fighting my bosses so much.

SAGE
Yes, because that will dissolve another illusion. We often think that whatever issue we have in the present has its roots in the present. But most of our present issues have roots far beyond the present. One must be willing to look deeper.
Why are you shouldering all this? Why is it important that others do things your way? Why do you have to have the answers for everyone else?

Dig deep. How does this issue with your school in your present life relate to something in your past? How does having the answers for others weave into your past wounds?

I

I never thought the two were connected before. Perhaps this fight has some childhood connections I did not notice before. As a kid, I did think I could control the outcome of everything in our house. Or at least, an impact on things. It was too scary to feel powerless. So, I believed if I did everything right, if I was the perfect kid, then I would have had a better childhood. My dad would have stayed. My parents would have loved me more.

It's why I was protective of my parents. No matter how bad it was, I had to believe I was at fault. That they were not to blame for anything. The opposite was too painful to even consider. If they were responsible for their actions, it was because I was unlovable. My dad left because I wasn't good enough. I wasn't valuable to him. I was unworthy of his love or his staying in my life.

So, I had to believe I had done something. Some action that pushed them away. It wasn't me; it was my behavior. That led me to develop all this control. If I controlled myself and everything around me, then nothing bad would happen. As if I was in control of my parents. As if I was in control of my world.

SAGE

That is the illusion of control. And why we attach to it so much as humans. Do you understand know that you were loveable as a child and you are loveable as an adult?

I
Yes. I think I can embrace that reality. My parents' actions reflected their wounding, not me. Still, that is a hard lesson to accept day in and day out. I find myself slipping into blaming myself sometimes.

SAGE
That is where daily self-reflection helps. We all slip. All of us. All the time. We are not perfect. The point is we are making progress. We identify when we are controlling and seek out the root.

Control is wanting what we do not have: control of people, places, and things. We want control of our world. But we do not have that. We are powerless over what others do. We are powerless over the world.

I
Does everything always lead back to childhood?

SAGE
Control always leads back to our wounding. Our pain. For many of us, that wounding started in childhood. But not always. But control always is based in fear of not being in control. And that terrifies us.

So, we do what you did. Fight the system. Rage against the machine. Take control by any means. Quit. Move somewhere else in search of utopia. Kill off our Higher Power and become god ourselves.

Doesn't work. And if we are lucky, at some point we will realize this fact. And stop fighting. Stop fighting others but mostly stop fighting ourselves.

EVERYTHING IS A SPIRITUAL ISSUE

I
I bet you have an answer to control?

SAGE
Of course, I do! There is a Buddhist philosophy that states that all physical ailments are because we are emotionally ill. And all emotional ailments are because we are spiritually ill. So, everything is a spiritual issue. And the answer to all ailments and ills is the Eleventh Step of Alcoholic Anonymous. Seek through prayer and meditation to improve your conscious contact with God, as you understand God.

I
I don't have a clue who God is. I don't even know if there is a God. Or if I want to believe in that!

SAGE
Each person must determine who "God" is for them. Study the sages and then trust your own intuition about this Higher Power. I believe the proof that there is an Ultimate Reality is this verse from the Book of Job:
"Can you command the sun to rise?
Can you show the dawn its place?"[27]
I cannot. I cannot cause the sun to rise. There must be a Higher Power, an Energy that causes the sun to rise each morning without fail. And that Higher Power isn't me!

---

[27] Book of Job 38:12

Each person will also have to determine what "God" does in this world. Again, study the sages and then trust your own intuition. Don't be afraid to let go of old definitions and embrace new ones.

Let's start with what God is not. For me, "God" is not a person. Certainly not the old man on a throne. God is not the savior or the fixer of all our problems. God is not the harsh judge waiting to send us all to hell.

For me, the Source of all Life is Energy. The Life Force that all in creation are a part of. Nothing exists apart from this Energy. Everything, every single part of creation is part of the Whole. Our task as humans is to remember this fundamental and essential truth.

I

I feel overwhelmed! This concept of God is too big for me to get a hold of.

SAGE

I agree! The totality of God is too big for us limited humans. All great spiritual seekers come to this realization. I will share with you two quotes that put this reality into perspective.

The German theologian Karl Rahner identified God as "an Incomprehensible Mystery." This Unknown One is beyond human understanding. And centuries before him, St. Augustine stated: "If we understand it, it is not God."

I

So, how do I wrestle with the question of who God is, if God is unknown and beyond me?

SAGE

One way I do it, is to break the totality of this Energy into parts that I call the Avatars of God.

THE AVATARS OF GOD

I
Avatars? Really?

SAGE

An "Avatar" is an incarnation or manifestation of the Deity. In this case, because the Source of All is too big for us to comprehend, we examine how the Source of Energy manifests on this planet and throughout our lives in a way that we can more easily grasp. For me, there is an Avatar for each of the chakras.

1. God is Ground.
    The Source of Life gives us our grounding.
    Our security, our spiritual and emotional balance.
2. God is Creativity.
    The Master of ingenuity, inspiration, originality.
    Creator of every single thing in existence.
3. God is Power.
    The Live Force generates influence over all.
    This Energy is the supreme Authority.
4. God is Love
    Love. Compassion. Empathy. Kindness.
    Empathy. Forgiveness. Openness.
5. God is Truth.
    I love Ghandhi's definition:
    "God is Truth. Truth is God."
6. God is Consciousness
    Wisdom. Reality. Knowledge.
7. God is Union.
    I am One with the One.
    I am One with the Whole.

EMBRACE SUFFERING

I

Even though I don't believe God is a "Father," I still get caught up in that image of God as a Parent. I still want "God" to love me. To protect me. To save me.

SAGE

That is common, especially for those of us raised in a Christian culture. I believe there are powerful lessons to glean as we move away from the illusion that some Heavenly Parent out there ready to save us.

First lesson. To believe that God will swoop in to save me without any action on my part is not anchored in adulthood. I believe it's more a partnership.

To quote AA: "If we are painstaking about this phase of our development, we will be amazed before we are half-way through.... We will realize that God is doing for us what we could not do for ourselves."[28] So, God will do for me what I cannot do for myself when I am painstaking about my spiritual development. I must change the things I can change: my thoughts, attitudes, my behaviors, my choices. That's the partnership.

Second lesson. There will be karma for thoughts and actions. Karma for my mistakes doesn't make me a "bad" person. Just a human person. So, when things go the opposite way I want, I need to first look and see if I have contributed to the outcome in some way. This is not about blame or masochism. It's about being responsible for my thoughts and behaviors and actions.

---

[28] https://aasantacruz.org/wp-content/uploads/2020/07/The-Promises.pdf Accessed December 12, 2023.

Sometimes if I dig a little bit, I can see exactly how my behavior led to whatever happened. For example, last week I found a big mess in the stockroom. I could have cleaned it up but I just didn't want to. So, I left it for someone else. What happened? The very next day, there is a huge mess at Guest Service: broken candles, spilled shampoo, frosting all over the counter, and carts of abandoned merchandise everywhere! There was no walking away because it was my job to clean it up!

Karma is a natural law on this planet. Because I believe in reincarnation, karma follows me through my lives. There is no escape from my responsibilities.

Third lesson. When challenging things happen, may our response be one of acceptance. We can only do the next right thing. We do not control the outcome.

Embracing the porcupine of suffering is so difficult because it will mean embracing pain and loss. And pain and loss are essential parts of life that convey great lessons We can only learn how to be brave through facing our fear. Only learn honor through facing our shame. Learn humility through facing our guilt. Learn gratitude through facing our grief.

For through suffering, we come to embrace the greatest gifts of our humanity. Courage. Strength. Fearlessness. Power. Compassion. Forgiveness. Trust. Wisdom. Acceptance. And then we come to know that we are indeed, one with the Source of Life. Because we are all those attributes and all those attitudes are "God."

I

That sounds like a great ending but the beginning and the middle sound daunting!

EMBRACING SCARS

SAGE

Let me share a great story that I heard at a grief support group. It's from a cartoon strip featuring farm animals. A donkey asks his friend the pig about his scars and is told "I got them when I lost someone I loved very much."

The donkey goes to the wisest animal on the farm and asks, "How can I avoid scars?"

The wisest says, "Don't love anyone. Stay isolated. Don't share your real self with anyone."

The donkey comes back to the pig, who asks, "Well?"

To which the donkey replied, "I'll take the scars."[29]

The point is, we need to love. To create. To risk. Yes, we may not succeed in the way we want. And we will get scars. But the alternative is to be dead while still breathing. To be walled up, isolated, so full of fear that we never venture into the realm of being truly human.

Yes, life is full of pain and suffering. And here's the ironic part. I have found the most fascinating, wise, courageous, and insightful people have the most scars. Because they have lived and loved and lost and learned. And have embraced being fully alive!

---

[29] Bob Bartlett, conversation with author, October 21, 2023, from cartoon strip in Star Tribune, author unknown.

CLOSEST TO GOD

SAGE

Here's another story that may illuminate you regarding the point of suffering. Guru Neem Karoli Baba was approached by a woman who told him of all her pain. She asked him, "Do you ever suffer like this?"

He replied, "Yes, I suffer greatly. I have emotional pain and physical illness that cause me great suffering."

She told him, "Isn't it terrible to suffer so much?'

To which Maharaj Jia replied, "No. It is when I suffer that I am closest to God."

Each person has full power over how to handle suffering. Will I be resentful and blaming? Will I wallow in self-pity? Will I deny my pain and escape any hint of suffering? Will I say "Fuck You to everyone and everything, including God?

Will I accept what I cannot control of the outcome and embrace suffering as the cost of being human? Will I surrender and seek the gifts of suffering?

A long time ago at St. John's University, my professor told the story of a woman who was dying from a painfully terminal cancer. There was no cure. No hope. She told him: "All I can do is sit here and let God love me."

Will I do the same in the midst of my suffering?

OSLO

I
So, I need to seek the opposite of pain to get to love? The opposite of fear to get to courage?

SAGE
It's not about dualism. I had a spiritual experience last year that demonstrated the reality that dualism is not the answer. Because nothing exists apart from God. Nothing!

On a recent trip to Norway, we went to the Oslo Opera House. Beautifully situated on the Norwegian Sea. As I was having a quiet moment, energetically the water in the middle of the bay began to churn. And suddenly out of the water came this incredibly wild creature. I could only think of the Tasmanian Devil from a childhood cartoon. Later I realized it was a troll, the mythical creature of Norway. Swinging around, this ferocious beast faced me and said, "I am Fear. Wanna play?"

"I don't think so." I said shakily.

"Why not?"

"I don't know who you are."

"Yes, you do" He challenged me.

"I don't trust you." I admitted.

Immediately, Fear shapeshifted from this devilish wild character into what I can only describe as Bliss. I stood in amazement because I knew this Bliss was God. The Source of Life. Wisdom. The One.

Bliss said, "I am all things. I am Fear when I need to teach you Bravery. Shame to teach Honor. Guilt to teach Humility. Grief to Gratitude. Lies to Truth. Illusions to Reality. All are all part of Me. Fear is not separate from Me. Fear is not the antithesis of Me. We are the Same."

"I know that." I mumbled.

"Then embrace it deeper. Know it stronger. Know it clearer. Know it in very cell of your Being. Nothing, absolutely nothing, exists apart from Me. I am Everything. Everything is Me.

With that, Bliss disappeared.

I

Wow. That sounds scary and sacred all at the same time. But I am beginning to understand that this is probably true for everything on the spiritual path. A mixture of scary and sacred.

SAGE

That is a very wise statement! I totally agree. That is why it is so important to face ourselves. Knowing who we are is essential to accepting and surrendering to this path that will shake us. Terrify us. And at the same time, call us. Draw us. Invite us. Welcome us to come home. Home to True Selves.

I

I know that's what I want. But how do I do it?

THE GIFT OF SURRENDER: COMING HOME

SAGE
It's a process. A process of ups and downs and backwards and forwards and insides and outsides. Pay attention. Listen. Trust your truth. You know the way.

I
How about some practical tips?

SAGE
Our egos are on the surface of the personality and our true Self is at the core.[30] So, one of my tasks as an adult is to identify where and when and how emotion is running my life. Where am I running away in fear or addiction? Where is my shame overwhelming me? When does guilt push me away from being accountable? When have I abdicated my responsibility? Who am I blaming?

When I feel like the world is hurting me, the opposite is the truth: I am hurting the world. I am hurting both myself and those around me. And ultimately, I am hurting the world.

I
I am beginning to see the progress. I want to think that all my decisions only affect me. And if I try hard enough to hide the decisions that are not wise, I can stay in the illusion that my decisions only affect me. But I know my decisions, wise and unwise, do affect others. My family. My school. My friends. And I see that even a greater circle is affected.

---

[30] Eknath Easwaran, translator, The *Bhagavad Gita,* Blue Mountain Mediation Center, Tamales, CA, 2007, 86.

SAGE

Another practical attitude I have been working on is to tame my ego. I try to shift from being god in my world to being me in God's world.

I try every day to surrender my ego. Let go of my control. Yield to my Higher Power. Continue to learn how to be what I am: a wonderful and imperfect human being. A gifted and flawed creature.

I am not the Force that commands this planet. At my core, I am part of that Force but not the totality of that Force. So, humility demands I realize my place in the cosmos. And that God, however you define "God," is the Ultimate Force. I am one drop of water in the Ocean of the Whole.

I

How do I learn that? What do I do?

SAGE

One of the most important spiritual practices is that of solitude. Being alone. Then you can listen. For all of us, listening is scary. And yes, sacred. It's when we are all alone with ourselves, that we can see and hear our egos. Our fear. It's when we can see or hear God. When there are no outer distractions. Solitude terrifies us so we stay busy, doing all sorts of things to avoid ourselves. The paradox is we must be alone to realize we are connected!

I

I want to circle back to a story you told me a while ago. You said you envisioned yourself on a different planet and were sitting on the shore eating rocks and dirt and grass. But there was a perfectly good pizza beside you that you couldn't eat. Did you ever figure out how to eat the pizza?

EMBRACING THE PORCUPINE

SAGE

Oh, that took me years to figure that one out! I'd like to tell you I got the answers in a thunderbolt. But the insights came to me much slower. It was only after exhaustion from wrestling with myself, I finally surrendered to acceptance.

This is the spiritual journey. Climbing the mountain or swimming the ocean (whichever analogy you like) is time-consuming, labor-intensive, shake-you-to-the- core hard work. You don't get to the top or the opposite shore magically. You get there one step at a time. One stroke at a time.

Everyone has a pizza in front of them that they can't or won't eat. We are all eating rocks and dirt and grass. Perhaps it's a relationship that is harmful to us. Or an endeavor we are called to embark upon but are saying "no." Or an amends we must make. Or an invitation from our Higher Power to walk closer. This is a learning planet, so we all have our own pizza in front of us. And we are refusing to eat it!

For years, I stared at the pizza, incapable of even picking up a piece. At first, I did what most of us do: Tried to stop eating rocks and dirt and grass., without investigating why I was eating rocks and dirt and grass. Finally, I asked myself the essential question: Why did I not pick up a piece of this gorgeous pizza?

The answer flabbergasted me: I didn't deserve the pizza; I deserved rocks and dirt and grass. I wasn't good enough for something fresh and tasty and mouth-watering and a whole lot healthier that rocks and dirt and grass. That realization humbled me. Then motivated me. So, even after years of therapy, I had yet another level of shame and pain to uncover and heal.

What propelled me forward was the reality that I have only so much room in my body. Our emotional wounds are not only firmly intrenched in the mind. They are embedded in the cells of our physical body. And they take up room! So, I can carry around my fear, shame, guilt, grief, lies, and illusions around with me. Or I can heal them. And then release them.

I

What happens then?

SAGE

A wonderful therapist who taught me that the principal benefit to healing was twofold. By facing my wounds — my fear, my shame, my guilt, my grief, my lies, my illusions, my attachments — I could heal them. That healing led to releasing the pain, so I no longer had to carry it. Then an amazing thing happens! I have more room for my soul![31]

I had more room in my mind and in my body for owning the reality that I am part of the Whole. I am not perfect and that's just fine! I am worthy. And valuable. I have been wounded and am flawed. Yet I am enough!

The more room there is for my soul, the more conscious I am. And that is the goal: to be conscious of who I am at my core in every minute of every day.

I

Is that Enlightenment?

SAGE

Yes. And everything in our lives is an invitation to move closer to Enlightenment or further away. To embrace that I am One with the Whole or reject that I

---

[31] Mary Anna Palmer. Psychotherapy session, 1997.

am One with the Whole. For a long time, working at Target was a formidable challenge. My reaction was to move away from Enlightenment. Move away from God. Move away from my True Self. As rage and resentment took over, I rejected every opportunity to learn any hint of insight.

I

But you faced yourself because you told me that you got glimpses of Enlightenment at Target.

SAGE

Yes, I finally got tired of getting hurt by the sharp quills and savage teeth of the porcupine. I quit fighting what I could not control. I sought solutions to the issues I could impact. The places in my life where I had a responsibility to act, I tried to do the next right thing. In short: I embraced the porcupine.

I am still at Target. With an adjusted attitude and behavior. And that has made all the difference. Embracing the porcupine meant I quit fighting the quills and teeth. I quit demanding that life work out as I command. I began to search for the gifts behind the quills of the porcupine. Amazingly, the less I fought, the more the porcupine became my friend.

I

Really? A friend?

SAGE

Yes. A friend. A teacher. There is no dualism. We are all teachers and learners in this incredible journey. As I embraced the porcupine, I sought my lessons. What was I at Target to learn? And the answer was that a great spiritual education awaited me a Target. If I was willing to learn.

Now, I seek the spiritual lessons of Target. I still fall backwards sometimes and that's okay. I get to be human. The point is my intention is on Enlightenment. I joked with a friend that she worked for God.[32] So, I describe my adventure at Target the same way. I work for God. Target just pays my salary.

I

I know we are coming to the end of our time together. I just want to say how grateful I am for your wisdom. I remember back to when I first met you and I was so scared. So unsure of myself. I didn't have a clue who I was. I am so grateful because you taught me the most valuable lesson of all. You have taught me how to find myself. How to accept myself. To be my True Self.

SAGE

All I did was walk beside you and share my experience. You did the hard work. You were brave enough to face your fears. Creative enough to face your shame. Humble enough to face your guilt. Grateful enough to face your grief. Honest enough to face your lies. Aware enough to face your illusions. Then you surrendered enough to be One with your Higher Self. As we part, I leave you with this.

> Wherever you go,
> whatever you do,
> whoever you are,
> whoever you become,
>> I will walk beside you
>> for as long as the Journey allows.

---

[32] Beth Mahutchin, conversation with author.

www.ingramcontent.com/pod-product-compliance
Lightning Source LLC
Chambersburg PA
CBHW070431010526
44118CB00014B/1997